All About Ferndale
Humboldt County, California
—Today—
A Victorian Village
A National Historical Landmark

"An Artistic Introduction"

Written & Illustrated by:
  Donna Setterlund
Miscellaneous Stories contributed by:
  The People of Ferndale & The Enterprise
Published by:
  Carriage House Studio Publications
  Ferndale, California
Edited and typeset by:
  Kaytis Advertising & Secretarial Services
  Ferndale, California
Printed by:
  Direct Impact, Rohnert Park, California

© 1989 First Edition; Carriage House Studio Publications
Ferndale, California 95536
Library of Congress Catalog Card # 89-85952
ISBN # 0-9624342-0-5
All rights reserved. No part of this publication may be reproduced or used in any form or by any means without permission from the author/publisher

Thank You

Thank you Ferndale folks, for sharing your town with me.

Thank you for creating the stories and for helping me gather the past and the present to put this book together. It is you, the people, who make our town what it is, and it is you, the people, about whom this book is written.

Thank you Cliff, my husband, and my family for supporting me and always being there during the endless days and nights while I painted and put the pieces together. Thank you most of all for loving me. It is this love which inspired me to create this book and the pictures within.

Dedication:

*To my family, especially my husband Cliff
and all of you who believe in me.*

Contents

Introduction to the Artist		4 & 5
Introduction to Ferndale		6 & 7
The Past Lives On		8
Chapter 1	"Ferndale, Pretty as a Picture" A picture tour of Ferndale featuring Victorian Homes, Churches, and Interesting Places	9
Chapter 2	"Main Street - Busy and Beautiful" Check out our Main Street with all of its Unique Shops, Stores, Businesses and People	33
Chapter 3	"Maps, Guides, Things to See and Do"	
	Area & City Maps	67
	Business Listings and Directory	72
	Guide: Things to See and Do	76
Chapter 4	"Meet our People" The inhabitants of Ferndale make the town. Take a look at some of our people ... we're proud of them	90
Chapter 5	"What's Cookin'?" Candy Shops, Restaurants, and where to get a quick snack	107
	Guide to Good Eating	108
Chapter 6	"A Place for the Night" Bed & Breakfast Inns, Hotels, and Camping	116
	Guide: Places to Stay	117
Chapter 7	"Industry, Our Valley, & Other Tidbits" The Dairy Industry, Ranches, Butterfat Palaces, and other Important Information	129
About the Prints	How you can order prints of the artwork in this book, including specifications	
	Order Form	143

Introduction

"An Inspiration of Love"

Hi, my name is Donna Setterlund. I am an Artist, a proud mother and a very happy wife. My life has been filled with the ups and downs that most everyone has, but my love for life and the world around me has always given me the inspiration to dream and create. Because I am a self-taught artist, it has taken me many years of trial and error to develop and cultivate a style with which I feel comfortable. Just being alive and experiencing life has been the best teacher of all. I have always loved the out-of-doors, animals, children, old houses and people with smiles. A picture says a thousand words, so I have painted Ferndale in pictures, doing what I love to do most - create.

When I started this project, I had no idea how much work I was getting myself into. The artwork and the stories were the easy part. Talking to the people and organizing was the hard part. I talked and asked questions and talked and waited and took notes and talked. Everyone was enthusiastic about the idea and concept of this project, but helping them make up their minds about what they really wanted to say in the book was difficult, to say the least.

Because this was my first experience with publishing, I really had lots of lessons to learn. I knew what I wanted my finished product to look like and I knew how I wanted to present the town, but how could I be fair to everyone? I tried newspaper ads and literature by mail with very little response, so I went back to talking to as many people as possible, one by one. Time was a very important factor and it kept ticking away no matter how hard I tried to hurry. My children had to adjust to Mom's moods — and my husband gave me my daily dose of courage to keep going. Things have a way of working themselves out and all the pieces started fitting together.

There is so much that makes up a town, and it is almost impossible to include everything and everyone. I have done my best.

This book is "An Inspiration of Love": the love of the people in our town, the love in the smiles on their faces, the love of old homes and buildings, the love of the values and old ideals that make our town special, and the love I feel as I share this world with you.

This book has been created for you with love.

Donna Setterlund

"An Introduction to Ferndale"

"Fern Dale", as it was first spelled, started to blossom in the late 1800's. Nestled in the Eel River Valley on the Lost Coast of Northern California, it lies quietly hidden — a quaint little Victorian Village saved from time and preserved with a splendor and uniqueness all its own. The throbbing heart of a lively dairy-rich valley, Ferndale was once affectionately referred to as the "Cream City". Mansions of Victorian architecture dot the patchwork-quilted fields surrounding the town. All who come to visit marvel at the beauty.

Almost lost in the devastating 1955 and 1964 floods, the people refused to let her die. A handful of imaginative citizens who loved the town started pulling together to fix up, paint up, and save the past — an act which birthed the thriving community of today. A melting pot of Scandinavian, Swiss-Italian and Portuguese cultures, individual and community festivals are celebrated throughout the year. Artists and Artisans ventured into Ferndale in the 1960's; some stayed and some left, but Ferndale remained interested in the Arts. Several galleries opened along with numerous stores selling unique goods — a community like no other was created. Visiting the town is like stepping back in time 100 years.

Ferndale", now preserved as a State Historical Landmark, continues to fascinate visitors who come to partake in her pleasures.

Old Timers still enjoy her streets — a lifestyle forgotten by so many is still lived here by her people.

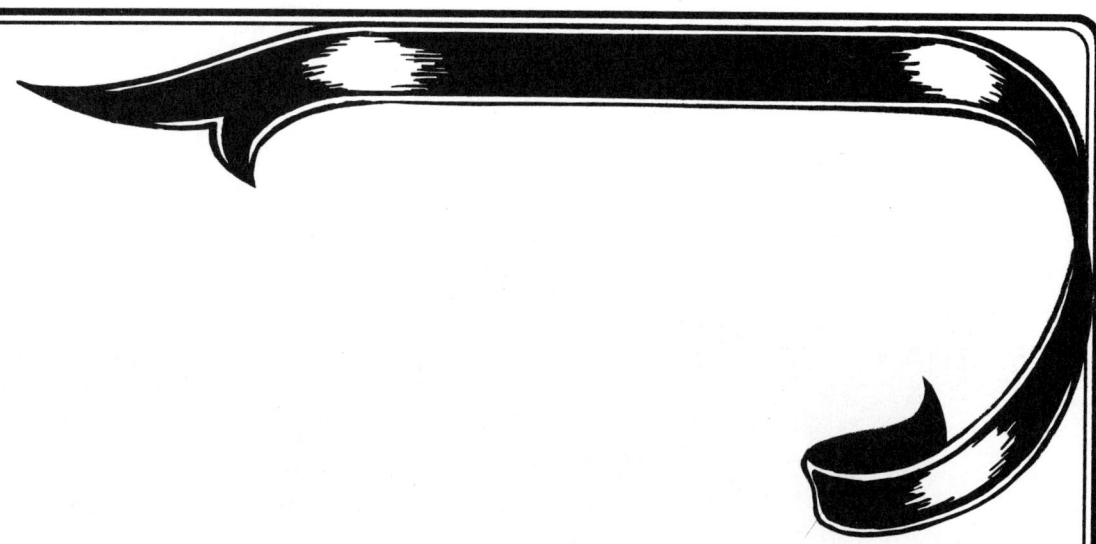

You can walk casually along Main Street and view the beautiful architecture. Stop in the shops and enjoy old-fashioned friendliness and merchandise from the past. You will find hand-made items created with love and a feeling of accomplishment that is shared by all.

Ferndale is primarily a residential town where families have an opportunity to grow together. The city's population has a modest but steady increase each year and is now about 1500, including approximately 3500 on adjacent farm lands. The city itself occupies approximately one square mile of a beautiful little valley, nestled up against the coastal hills.

Larger streams like the Bear and Mattole Rivers to the south and the Eel River provide many attractions for the sports fisherman. Catches range from early season trout and late summer half-pounders to the most exciting of them all, salmon and steelhead.

In this book you will share a small part of our world. Each person has done their own thing in representing their homes, businesses and families. Each page has become one little part of our community and when they are all put together we have what could be referred to as a "Pot-luck" Book. It has been compiled by one but created by many.

We are proud to share with you some of our treasures, our stories and our love.

Ferndale, 1909

"The Past Lives On"

As time passes us by and progress keeps us going onward, we don't often think of how we got to where we are and why we are here. The struggles and challenges of our forefathers should not be forgotten for they have created our present. In the Little Victorian Village of Ferndale we are proud of our past and our heritage and we try to keep its memory alive in our everyday lives. Our people love this town and we are proud to share our past and our present with those who wish to know.

"Our past lives on in our people today"

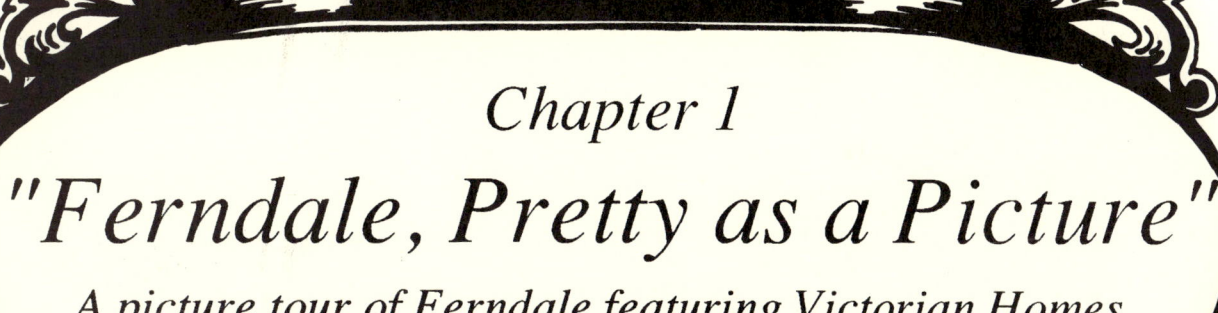

Chapter 1
"Ferndale, Pretty as a Picture"
A picture tour of Ferndale featuring Victorian Homes, Churches, and Interesting Places.

— Index —

	Print No.	Page
Fernbridge	#1011	10, 11
The Road to Ferndale	#1012	12, 13
Shaw House "Ferndale's Beginning"	#1014	14, 15
Victorian Beauties	#1016	16
Cowan's Corner	#1017	17
Old Hart House	#1018	18
Old Catholic Rectory	#1019	19
Main Street	#1021	20, 21
Thielman Home	#1022	22
Ben & Laura Liu Home	#1023	23
Berding Street	#1024	24
Lajoie Home	#1025	25
Church of the Assumption	#1026	26
First Congregational Church	#1027	27
McGee & Crlenjak	#1028	28
Francis Creek	#1029	29
Cemetary	#1030	30
Old Methodist Church	#1031	31
Smith Home (Barn at Christmas)	#1032	32

Fernbridge
"Gateway to Ferndale"

There she stands, a bridge across the years of time. Fernbridge, a bridge of dignity ... a bridge of integrity ... our bridge. Built in the Roman style, Fernbridge, was the longest reinforced concrete bridge in the world at the time of her dedication on November 16, 1911. An outstanding engineering feat ... an historic bridge.

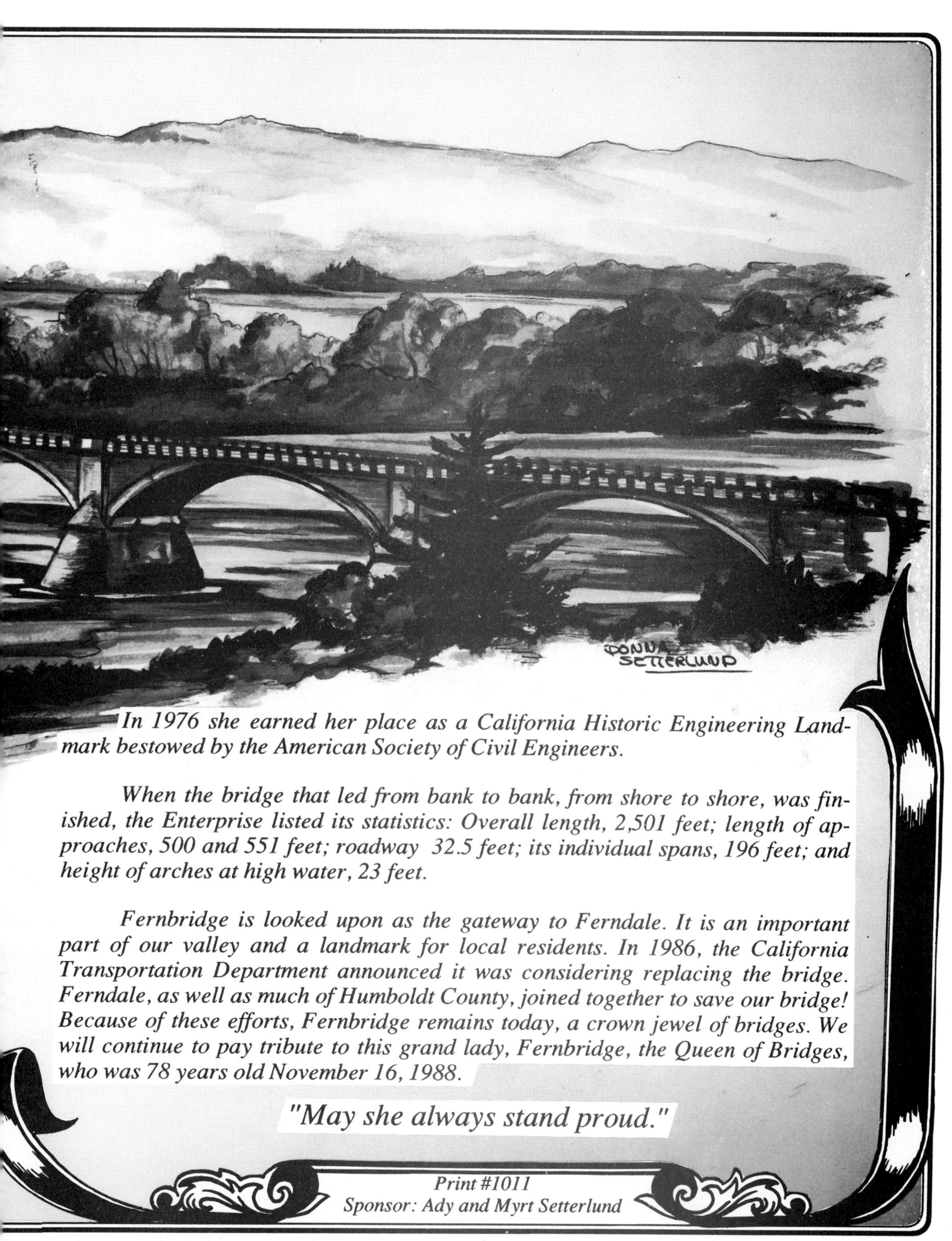

In 1976 she earned her place as a California Historic Engineering Landmark bestowed by the American Society of Civil Engineers.

When the bridge that led from bank to bank, from shore to shore, was finished, the Enterprise listed its statistics: Overall length, 2,501 feet; length of approaches, 500 and 551 feet; roadway 32.5 feet; its individual spans, 196 feet; and height of arches at high water, 23 feet.

Fernbridge is looked upon as the gateway to Ferndale. It is an important part of our valley and a landmark for local residents. In 1986, the California Transportation Department announced it was considering replacing the bridge. Ferndale, as well as much of Humboldt County, joined together to save our bridge! Because of these efforts, Fernbridge remains today, a crown jewel of bridges. We will continue to pay tribute to this grand lady, Fernbridge, the Queen of Bridges, who was 78 years old November 16, 1988.

"May she always stand proud."

Print #1011
Sponsor: Ady and Myrt Setterlund

"The Road to Ferndale"

After crossing Fernbridge you will find yourself in a valley dotted with wild flowers in the spring, and fields of lush green grass which provide the base for our prosperous dairy industry. In the distance you will begin to notice the towering steeples of the churches that nestle themselves in the safety of the surrounding hills. Clouds embrace the horizons. You have discovered a place out of story books, to be shared and experienced by all who come to find it.

Print #1012
Sponsor: Citizens Utilities of California

*As a proud member of our business community, **Citizens Utilities of California** would like to welcome you to our valley. You are on the road to a little Victorian Village like no other. We hope you enjoy your visit with us, as you see our sights and partake in our hospitality. "Welcome to Ferndale!"*

"The Shaw House"

The oldest remaining structure in Ferndale and the home of the community's founder, Seth Louis Shaw, the house is on the National Register of Historic Places as an outstanding example of Victorian Gothic Revival architecture.

In 1852, Seth Shaw and his brother, Stephen, who was California's first American artist in the gold rush, explored the country to determine if it had value. Until then, only the Indian population knew of the valley. They found their way into a prairie at a juncture of a stream now known as Francis Creek. Giant six-foot ferns were in quantity but no large trees remained standing. An old redwood which *had fallen and conveniently split into "planks" lent itself to their building efforts. A large earthen fireplace and chimney provided heat and cooking space.*

The Shaw brothers each claimed 160 acres of land and "Fern Dale" was born. Seth Shaw was a farmer, and he soon found the land was great for potatoes. His first income came from potatoes taken by canoe to Heney's Railroad and then to Heney's Landing on Humboldt Bay which were then shipped to market in San Francisco. Stephen Shaw was not to remain in the new settlement. He was an artist, not a farmer.

It didn't take long for the countryside to grow and in June of 1853 the first election was held with 21 voters casting ballots.

In 1854, Seth Shaw began construction of this substantial residence. By 1860, the home became Ferndale's first post office, and at the same time, the home was announced open to the traveler with an invitation to stop and enjoy the hospitality.

Seth Louis Shaw

Print # 1014
Sponsor: Ken and Norma Bessingpas

"Victorian Beauties"

Victorian architecture appears not only on Main Street, but all around the valley. Much of it was built in a rush in the late 1800's when merchant princes and dairy kings felt they should show their worth to the world. These Victorian structures adapted the popular Eastern styles of Gothic, Stick and Eastlake, and Queen Anne and then added their own personal touches. If you look closely you'll find there are no two alike.

This beautiful home is at 1249 Rose Avenue.

Print #1016
Sponsor: Carriage House Studio

"Cowan's Corner"

This home is a Queen Anne-Eastlake structure. The property was originally bought by J.H. Trost in March 1899. W.G. Dauphiny purchased the house in April, 1904 and occupied it until 1957. It has been referred to as "The Dauphiny House".

In 1987, while in the process of remodeling, a board was found in the kitchen with this inscription: "Ferndale's leading Painter and Decorator" signed: Thomas P. Wilson, dated" March, 1899.

The present owners are Robert G. and Dorothy J. Cowan who purchased the home in August, 1986 and affectionately refer to their place as "Cowan's Corner".

Print #1017
Sponsor: Robert & Dorothy Cowan

"Old Hart House"

This showboat house on Main Street was built by Manual Brasil in 1885. The architectural style is non-symmetrical Italianate with Queen Anne oriel or bay windows, a mixed style with a low-pitched roof.

The home was purchased by Attorney Plummer Frederick Hart in 1894. Hart's daughter, May, married Joseph Armitage Shaw, son of Seth Shaw, and lived in the home until her death. The place was then purchased by Dr. Francis Bruner, who operated it as the town hospital from 1915 to 1920.

In recent years the home has been repainted and restored by the present owners, Mr. and Mrs. John Wunderlich.

Print #1018
Sponsor: Mr. & Mrs. John Wunderlich

"Old Catholic Rectory"

The old Catholic Rectory, 563 Ocean Avenue, was built in the Stick and Eastlake style in 1884 with George F. Costerisan as the architect. It was the rectory of the Catholic Church of the Assumption for 80 years before it was moved to its present site in 1964, where it was surrounded by an old fashioned fence of square pickets. It has been completely restored and is a culturally important building. The parish priest provided advice, comfort and help in times of trouble and refuge to those in need. In the early 1960's when the proposal was made to demolish the building, it was met with strong opposition, including impassioned letters to the Pope. Present owners are John and Joan Rutherford.

Print # 1019
Sponsor: John and Joan Rutherford

"Main Street"

Print #1021
Sponsor: Carriage House Studio

"Thielman Home"
1337 Lincoln Street

This Victorian home was built around the turn of the century. It is currently owned by Bill Thielman and Patty Purvis-Thielman, Co-Owners of "The Fern Cafe."

Print #1022
Sponsor: Bill Thielman and Patty Purvis-Thielman

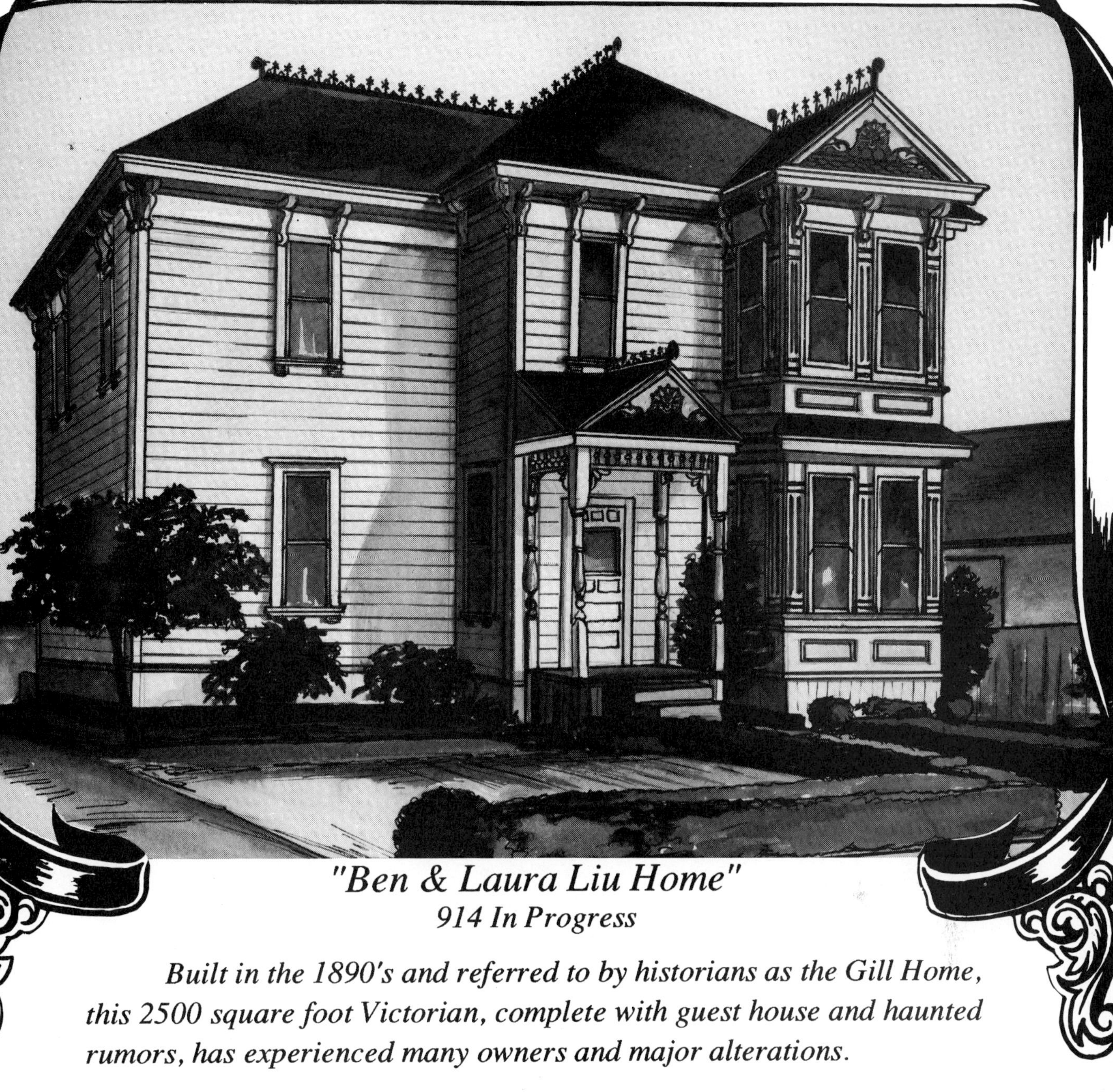

"Ben & Laura Liu Home"
914 In Progress

Built in the 1890's and referred to by historians as the Gill Home, this 2500 square foot Victorian, complete with guest house and haunted rumors, has experienced many owners and major alterations.

Purchased in 1985 by Ben and Laura Liu, countless weekend and after-work hours have been spent remodeling the interior to their satisfaction. Refinishing rustic redwood beams, which replace three bearing walls that were partially removed in the 1970's was just one challenging project. Other interior improvements included a complete kitchen remodel, floor refinishing, and extensive wallpapering & painting.

Plans to replace all destroyed gingerbread and exterior features to its originality is an exciting project that will soon be underway.

Print #1023
Sponsor: Ben & Laura Liu

"Berding Street"

Just one short block from and parallel to Main Street, Berding Street is a showplace of stately Victorians. An easy walk beginning on Ocean or Shaw will carry you by colorful homes surrounded by lovely picture-perfect gardens. Don't miss it!

Print # 1024
Sponsor: Andy McBride

"Lajoie Home"
420 Berding Street

Known as the "Little Red School House" this home was built in 1868. The new owners, Ron and Philaine Lajoie, are in the process of interior and exterior restoration. Plans include extensive use of brick pathways encompassed by beautiful rose gardens.

Print #1025
Sponsor: Ron & Philaine Lajoie

"Church of the Assumption"

Print #1026
Sponsor: Father Doyle

The First Congregational Church of Ferndale
(Independent-Evangelical)
712 Main Street

With early beginnings in 1875, the church was founded March 17, 1876. The sanctuary was built in the style of New England Congregational Churches and was dedicated July 24, 1881. It was built on land purchased from Mrs. Isabella Shaw. The Honorable Joseph Russ donated the lumber, the 500 pound steeple bell and paid off one-sixth of the entire debt. The stained glass windows in the steeple are original and are lit at night. The interior of the sanctuary was remodeled in 1923-24 and in 1954, when a pillared portico and the Fellowship Hall also were added. A 1926 Pipe Organ with 10 ranks of 701 pipes was purchased in 1956 and restored in 1988. Over the years the church has become a community church. It became indepdent in 1974 and had mergers in 1949-52 and 1987.

Print # 1027
Sponsor: Pastor David Kilmer

Print #1028
Sponsors: Jack Crlenjak & Gerry McGee

"Francis Creek"

View of section of Francis Creek between the homes of Stan and Judy Dixon and the Crlenjaks. Amy and Michele Crlenjak acting their ages above the natural rock retaining wall.

Print #1029
Sponsor: Jack Crlenjak

"Protestant Cemetary"

Print #1030
Sponsor: John & Joan Rutherford

"Old Methodist Church"

Ferndale's first church. From 1858-60 the congregation was served by a monthly circuit rider. By 1860, it had acquired its own pastor and by 1873, a church had been built on the present site. In 1897, the original church was replaced by the present structure. Dedicated June 10, 1901, it was described as "one of the most beautiful churches in the county". The building, now privately owned by Clay & Paula Frazier, will house the Watkins & Frazier Cabinet & Furniture Making Shop. The interior of the church is being restored and the sanctuary will be open for visitors.

Print #1031
Sponsors: Clay & Paula Frazier

"Smith Home"

This country home, built in 1911, has been occupied by the Smith family since 1977.

Don & Michelle, who are both involved in the commercial fishing industry, wish the community holiday greetings with their annual Christmas display featuring a Christmas tree of fish floats surrounded by several package toting Christmas crabs as well as Santa and his sleigh pulled by eight dancing dolphins. The Smith's barn is used as a sign board for various occasions and passersby delight at their displays.

Print #1032
Sponsor: Tony & Dorothy Lorenzo

Chapter 2

"Main Street — Busy & Beautiful"

	Business Number	Print Number	Page
Victorian Village Inn	1	#1035	34,35
Bank of Loleta/U.S. Bank	4	#1036	36
Toles -N- Things	10	#1037	37
The Palace	11	#1038	38
Candy Stick Gallery	12	#1039	39
Mathes Jewelry	16	#1040	40
Hobart Galleries	17	#1041	41
Village Florist	18	#1042	42
Ferndale Books	19	#1043	43
Golden Gait Mercantile	21	#1044	44
Golden Gait Mercantile	21	#1045	45
I.O.O.F. Building		#1046	46
Perleeta's Doll House	24	#1047	47
Parlor Crafts	23	#1048	48
The Gazebo	30	#1049	49
Daves Saddlery	31	#1050	50
Abraxas	33	#1051	51
Village Art Glass	37	#1052	52
Sweetness & Light	60	#1053	53
Public Restrooms	62	#1054	54
Etters Victorian Glass	66	#1055	55
Tuzzy Muzzy	67	#1056	56
Gepettos	68	#1057	57
Nilsen Company	72	#1058	58
Lentz Department Store	73	#1059	59
Bank of America	75	#1060	60
Rings Pharmacy	77	#1061	61
Withywindle	78	#1062	62
Eifert Gallery	82	#1063	63
The Enterprise	84		64
NOTOCO Building	93	#1065	65
Carriage House Antiques	92	#1066	66

#1 Victorian Village Inn

Ferndale's largest commercial structure, built in 1890 by Ira Russ, which was, and still is, considered one of Humboldt County's most beautiful Victorians, has come to life again as the Victorian Village Inn. The integrity of this century old building has been preserved through thoughtful restoration.

Print # 1035
Sponsor: Victorian Village Inn

Bank of Loleta - U.S. Bank of California

At the turn of the century, the Dickson and Dickson General Merchandise store in Loleta served as a hub for the business concerns of the farmers and ranchers of the immediate area. Tired of battling poor roads and constant flooding to reach the banks in Eureka, the people turned to the Dicksons to provide safekeeping for their hard-earned cash. They provided this service to their customers free of charge. A separate bank ledger was maintained to record deposits and withdrawals.

As cash accumulated, a more formal banking business developed. The Dicksons began to invest for their customers and to offer loans. Business continued in this fashion until the state of California halted private banking, requiring the Dicksons to incorporate, sell stock, and receive a state charter. In 1910, the Bank of Loleta was capitalized.

It wasn't until the mid-seventies that the Board of Directors changed focus, hired Bruce Roberts as president, and began a vigorous growth stategy. Several branches were added, including this Ferndale Branch. It is a statement of the Bank's strong community focus that the architecture is so authentically Victorian even though the structure was built in 1976! As a tremendously successful community bank, Bank of Loleta has a long history of being unique. That distinction still continues after its acquisition by U.S. Bancorp in 1988.

Print # 1036
Sponsor: U.S. Bank of California

#10 "Toles -N- Things"

This business originated in 1979 in Red Bluff, by the husband & wife team of George and Jean Pacheco. It was like a dream come true when they were able to buy this shop in 1986 and move to Ferndale.

While George keeps the saws buzzing, Jean keeps the paint flying. She paints for the shop, does special designs on commission and teaches the Folk Art form to interested and anxious students. They both love the challenge of "special requests." They will ship anywhere UPS or USPO will deliver.

In addition to the wood and folk art supplies, they carry a nice selection of Redwood gift items. And you have to see their "Blue Ribbon" winner "Cow Pie" to believe it. Children and adults are always impressed with the beautifully made doll houses. Mail can be directed to P.O. Box 56, Ferndale, California, 95536.

Print # 1037
Sponsor: George & Jean Pacheco

#11 "The Palace"

Built in the 1890's, the building has always housed a saloon, a favorite gathering place for celebrations, impromptu barbecues and feasts of steamed clams. The original bar is still in place. Owned and managed by Wayne Rocha and Mike Manzi, the tradition of hospitality continues. It is a part of Ferndale tradition.

Print # 1038
Sponsors: Wayne & Mike

#12 "Candy Stick Gallery"

The Candy Stick Building, built around 1900, was originally a candy store. In 1962, Viola Russ McBride, by then recognized as a fine artist, purchased the building for a gallery and art studio. She named it the Candy Stick because of the candy she had purchased there as a child.

Many artists have found their inspiration in the beauty of Northern California, particularly in Ferndale. The gallery gives these artists a chance to show their talents. Not only does the gallery feature 20 of Humboldt County's finest artists, but also represents 15 artisans who design hand crafted jewelry from around the world.

Print # 1039
Sponsor: Candy Stick Gallery

#16 "Mathes Jewelers"

Established over a century ago, Mathes Jewelers is the oldest jewelry store in Humboldt County and has been in the present location since 1920. The Observatory Clock on the sidewalk has been a landmark for 68 years. The business enjoys a reputation for excellence in watch and clock repair and the sale of fine traditional jewelry. Present owners, Virginia and Jack McDonald of Ferndale, will continue the tradition of service and value.

Print # 1040
Sponsor: Jack & Virginia McDonald

#17 "Hobart Gallery"

Hobart Gallery has been in existence for more than a quarter of a century, making it the oldest California art gallery north of San Francisco. It has been a representative of the North Coast Artists in paintings, pottery, and sculpture. Upstairs museum tours are available by appointment. The gallery has exhibited the work of artists with a great deal of pride and enjoyment, feeling as did Renoir that the nicest compliment to an artist is to buy his work.

Print # 1041
Sponsor: Hobart Brown

VILLAGE FLORIST

#18 "Village Florist"

Looking for an occupation that would provide an interesting future, Pam Milburn bought the Village Florist. That was in 1979, and with the help of friends like Marnie Phillis and Larry Martin, Pam learned the business.

Yes indeed, it has blossomed into a very unique little gift shop featuring flowers for every occasion. Fresh flowers, dried flowers, live plants and silk plants are very popular. You will also find balloons, country hats decorated with dried flowers, baskets, cards, wine gift items and many novelty items.

Pam says sometimes it's even a do-it-yourself florist, so if you need that special gift, just stop by and see what you can find, or create.

Print # 1042
Sponsor: Pam

#19 Ferndale Books

Ferndale Books has occupied the building at 405 Main Street since 1981 and is owned by Carlos & Marilyn Benemann. It has a general stock of over 25,000 out-of-print books.

The variety of subjects astound and the treasures found on the shelves delight all who browse through the store. If you are unable to find what you are looking for, Ferndale Books and it's Eureka store provide a search service. The store specializes in history and poetry and books about travel, California, and America, and also stocks new local history and natural history books.

The building itself was the site of two stores, which were destroyed by fire, and replaced by the present building in 1920.

Print # 1043
Sponsor: Carlos & Marilyn Benemann

#21 "The Golden Gait Mercantile"

Our store is one of the early Victorian commercial structures built in 1889. We are still supplying products treasured now and then.

Print # 1044
Sponsor: Marlin & Sandy Mesman

#21 "The Golden Gate Mercantile"

The wooden floors still squeak as you walk through the store and penny candy is still a penny. Whether you spend a few minutes or a few hours in our store, you'll find things you didn't know were still available. If you still believe red suspenders are to hold up your pants and that Cloverine Salve heals everything, you can find these necessities along with unusual hats, spices, moustache wax, penny candy, long johns, pots and pans. If you take the stairs to the second floor, you will find a free museum, showing a lifestyle of many years past, along wih antique furniture and other treasures. Truly a store in a town where there's something for everyone, just waiting, 100 years in the past, for you.

Print # 1045
Sponsor: Marlin & Sandy Mesman

"I.O.O.F. Building"
& the Boardwalk "Hall Shops"

#22 "Ferndale Bath Works"

A personal care bath, beauty & gift shop featuring custom filled baskets, world wide specialties, pot pourri, custom scenting, and items from Humboldt County including a full bath line. You will also find a collection of Ferndale Bath Works' own personal line of scents and bath care items. These and more in a unique little shop nestled in the heart of Ferndale's Main Street.

#24 "Perleeta's Doll House"

Old and new dolls and all their needs including repair & doll dressing, as well as vintage clothing.

#25 "Stan Bennett Motion Sculpture"
Since 1968.

"All my life I've been interested in the way things work, and kinetic sculpture is the natural result of combining design and mechanics. A sense of humor helps, too; I want my sculptures to be as much fun to own as they are to make."

#26 "G. Copeland Design Studio's Gallery"

Within the elegant French Victorian atmosphere of the North Coast's only "Wearable Art" Gallery, you will find: Exotic designer jewelry ... one-of-a-kind batiked and hand-painted men's, women's, and children's garments and accessories ... romantic Victorian gifts ... original multi-media works of art ... and a fascinating array of unique treasures. Visit us on the Boardwalk Arcade at 425 Main, directly behind Ferndale Bath Works.

#23 Parlor Crafts

The most complete needle craft store on the north coast. Also featuring a large selection of hand made items for your enjoyment. See page 48 for complete story.

Print # 1046
Sponsor: I.O.O.F. Building Shops

#24 "Perleeta's Doll House"

Perleeta's has antiques and beautiful collectible dolls. She has been in the doll business for 18 years and in Ferndale since 1980. She not only sells, but she appraises dolls, repairs dolls, and provides antique doll dresses, as well as takes her dolls to shows. She also has doll buggies from time to time and other novelties. Her new sideline is collectibles, figurines, cobalt blue glass, old banks, salt and pepper shakers, vintage clothing, linens, lace, and turn-of-the-century jewelry.

Print # 1047
Sponsor: Pearl Virgil

#23 "Parlor Crafts"

Parlor Crafts is the most complete needleart collection on the North Coast, featuring a complete line of counted cross stitch and needlepoint. We have over 2000 titles of books, the most up to date fabric selection, and what we don't have, we will order for you. Among our book selection, there are quilting, plastic canvas, crochet, knitting, hardanger, wood cut outs, needlepoint, and a sampling of many other craft books and patterns.

We also feature beginning classes in counted cross stictch, stitching on linen, needlepoint, and other classes.

Print # 1048
Sponsor: Stephanie Koch

#30 "The Gazebo"

The Gazebo building was built in 1898 in the Eastlake-Stick style, a fine example of Victorian architecture. It was first known as the Red Star Clothing Store run by Lee Taubman, and the Kausen family lived upstairs. Later, the first floor became Walter Vurrill's Candy Store and Ice Cream Parlor.

Since 1977, the Mellons have been the proprietors of the Gazebo, a shop filled with many decorative accessories and furniture. The shop highlights a country theme in Americana folk art as well as Scandinavian and English crafts.

Print # 1049
Sponsors: Paul, Suzannah and Paige Mellon

#31 "Dave's Saddlery"

"Today"

Dave's Saddlery is the last of the Western stores on the North Coast that still builds saddles and repairs boots. We are a full service western store offering boots, hats, jeans, and outwear for the entire family. The offering of good service and courteous help is the backbone of this business.

Dave's Saddlery stocks the clothes that folks in Humboldt County love to wear featuring such lines as: Tony Lama, Justin, Stetson, Woolrich, & Pendleton.

"Yesteryear"

The Building has always been used for the purveying of dry goods of one sort or another, starting with the Kausen & Williams Hardware store.

Print # 1050
Sponsor: Dave's Saddlery

#33 "The Abraxas Leather Shop"

The Old Red Front Store, built in 1898 by Peter Lund, has served a variety of uses. Some of these include a candy and cigar store, bicycle shop, paint shop, and variety store.

"Abraxas", a greek word signifying the forces of good and evil, is the building's most recent title. The store, owned by Kevin and Chris Boynton, displays brilliant gold and sterling jewelry, fine leather purses and pouches, pottery, both stained and blown glass, crafts, wooden boxes, clay figurines, and framed calligraphy. A diversity of artists, local and foreign, fill the Abraxas.

Print # 1050
Sponsors: Kevin and Chris Boynton

#37 "Village Art Glass"

For over ten years Village Art Glass has been executing outstanding stained glass art panels for customers all over the United States and in many foreign countries.

We take great pride in our original designs, tailored to the particular needs and choices of our customers, and to the superb quality of our craftsmanship, which guarantees the life and beauty of our work.

Design work by: Jo Bush
Craftsman: Jay Oxley

Print #1052
Sponsor: Jay Oxley

#60 "Sweetness and Light"

The sight, fragrance, and taste of fine traditional chocolates lives on at Sweetness and Light. Located next to the post office, our candy kitchen and store carry on a tradition that goes back to the turn of the century with Burrill's Confectionary and Ice Cream Fountain which later became Mill's Candies. All of Mills candies were produced and hand dipped by Miss Alma Jacobsen, a danish candy maker. Our village has another famous candy maker, our own Louise Goff, who has been making candies for more than 60 years.

We still cook our candies in small batches in copper kettles and work them on marble slabs. We use fresh local butter, real cream, real fruit flavors, and the best chocolate. On many week-days you can observe Ferndale's Candy Lady, Louise Goff, and her helpers dip each piece by hand sitting at a table in front of our big kitchen window. We enjoy making delicious chocolates and candies and hope that you enjoy every bite.

Print # 1053
Sponsor: Sweetness and Light

62 "Public Restrooms"

Winner in the "Places to Go In America" contest sponsored by 120 day PLUS Automatic Toilet Cleaner. Won in Entertainment/Transportation category. We the people of Ferndale are proud of our Victorian Restrooms. Materials and labor were donated by community members. We all stop by at special times to enjoy it's hospitality.

Print # 1054
Sponsors: Women's, Thomas Seymour; Men's, Marlene S. True

#66 "Etters Victorian Glass"

The building was constructed circa 1890. Originally located between the present buildings of Dave's Saddlery and the Abraxas, it was moved to it's present location around 1900. There it became Ferndale's sole harness shop for approximately 20 years. The shop was operated by members of the Kausen family and called the Grey Horse Harness Shop. By 1920, the harness making had ceased and a jewelry store opened — closing after a short time. It was followed by a paint store operated by Hall Jorgensen.

About 1935 E. Calanchini opened a shoe factory on the premises; it stayed in operation through the 1960's. Upon closing, the building saw an antique shop and second hand business. In 1970 Bill and Cheryl Etter purchased the building opening a picture frame and antique restoration shop operating to the present. It is interesting to note that there has been a picture frame business operating continuously in Ferndale since 1873.

Print # 1055
Sponsor: Bill Etter

#67 Tuzzy Muzzy

Tuzzy Muzzy: literally the two words mean "bunch of" and "mixed up". Since this was to be a family run store we wanted to have things that appealed to lots of different people, so we decided this was the name for us.

We have a wonderful assortment of gift items from Hummels to stickers, collectibles, dolls, crystal, and figurines. We also have cards, wrapping paper, silk flowers, candles, and more. Christmas is special here and you will find a winter fantasy and over a dozen trees filled with decorations. We hope you like our Tuzzy Muzzy of gifts and enjoy your visit to Ferndale.

Print # 1056
Sponsor: Susie Huckaby

#68 "Geppeto's"

At one time a drug store and barber shop welcoming young and old, the back of the barber shop also housed a bathtub. Cowboys, in from the hills, bought their once-a-month bath and haircut.

Today the building holds a shop with nostalgic toys, cards, and gifts. The favorite phrase heard in the store is "I remember that from when I was a kid!" Geppetto's still loves to welcome young and old with a laugh, fun, or building a memory, or even a bathtub toy.

Print # 1057
Sponsor: Gwen Roberts

#72 "Nilsen Co."

Opened in 1896 and considered one of Humboldt Counties oldest businesses, Nilsen Company began as a grocery and mercantile store.

Print # 1058
Sponser: Jeff Nilsen

73 "Lentz Department Store"

Lentz Department Store, where service comes first, is a family store, carrying something for everyone. Lentz's has been on Main Street for over 50 years. The store was started in 1948 by Ulice Lentz who ran it for 25 years and then sold it to Bernice Petersen who ran it for 15 years. Bernice's niece, Polly Stemwedel, bought the store in November 1988 after the death of her aunt. The store will continue to be called Lentz's after the original owners.

We've become a family tradition, from our storybook corner to our name-brand merchandise. For the women we carry a large selection of Graff, Pykettes, Ship 'N Shore and, new to us this fall will be Alfred Dunner. We're told we have the largest selection of sweaters year round. For the baby and toddlers we have Buster Brown Playwear—a must for the active child; you can find mens workshirts and socks in a large variety; for the handy homemaker, a large selection of notions and craft projects; and last but not least, we carry yardage and lace for your sewing needs.

Stop by and sign our guest book—it's fun to see what parts of the country our visitors hail from and we enjoy visiting with everyone.

Print # 1059
Sponsor: Polly Stemwedel

#75 "Bank of America"

Bank of America NT & SA purchased Russ-Williams Banking Company on June 29, 1935 and Ferndale Bank on December 28, 1936. The bank has conducted its Ferndale operation at 394 Main Street since it purchased the Russ-Williams Banking Company in 1935.

Dolores Rogers, Manager, and her staff, Carol Gibson, Sheri Shaw, Margarette Batten, Mary Katri, and Lois Lentz are available six days a week to provide customers with convenient banking services.

Print # 1060
Sponsor: B of A

#77 "Rings Pharmacy"

There has always been a Rings Pharmacy in Ferndale, it seems, with its towering false front, built in 1894-95 as a commercial Eastlake/Stick structure. J.H. Ring retired and passed on the business to his son, Meredith; the Ring family lived above the store.

Robert and Doris Nairne have had the pharmacy since 1968. Bob works from a large pharmacy in the rear and Doris presides over the front with stocks of everything from postcards to band-aids, including cosmetics, film, sunglasses and even old-fashioned personal service. "We don't have volume, we have variety," Doris says. If you don't see it, just ask, it may be in a drawer. They have a little bit of everything.

Print # 1061
Sponsors: Robert and Doris Nairne

#78 Withywindle

Withywindle specializes in quality stoneware, porcelain, jewelry, blown glass, wearable art, exotic woods and forged iron, by local artist craftsmen, including Dee who has worked in clay for almost 20 years and Milo, who has been blacksmithing and teaching equally as long.

You will find a wonderful variety of hand made items, from unusual stoneware goblets to honey pots. Each item varies from all others due to firing and artistic license. Please stop by to see our selection. We accept custom orders.

Print # 1062
Sponsor: Dee Johnson

#82 "The Eifert Gallery"

The Eifert Gallery is the main exhibit space of Larry Eifert and Carrie Grant, although their work is in other galleries. In their travels aboard their 40' yacht "October", they have discovered other artists whose works fit the the artistic feeling of the gallery; and, with several local artists, round out the group of about one dozen. The intention of The Eifert Gallery is to create a place where one may be surrounded by a feeling of clean quality and clear vision that portrays nature.

Print # 1063
Sponsor: Larry Eifert

#84 "The Ferndale Enterprise"

The Ferndale Enterprise was founded as a weekly newspaper in 1878 by the three young sons of the Methodist minister and sold by them when they moved with their father to another town. Since then, it has had 21 different publishers, many of them the same, as partnerships were formed and reformed.

George Waldner bought into the Enterprise in 1935, became sole owner and published the newspaper until 1977, its longest period under a single owner. His widow, Hazel Waldner, published The Ferndale Enterprise until 1980.

The present owner, Elizabeth Poston McHarry, bought the Ferndale Enterprise in 1982 from Marilyn Lidner. Under her unrelenting series of stories, editorials and state-wide publicity, along with the help of many interested and concerned residents of Humboldt County, Fernbridge across the Eel River was saved from destruction and named to the National Register of Historic Places.

In 1896, the Ferndale Enterprise was moved to its present site; today's building being constructed a number of years later. It is the oldest continuously operated newspaper in Northern California and among the oldest in the state. It has always served not only Ferndale, but the Eel River and Mattole Valleys.

#93 "660 Berding Street" The Assembly

Originally built in 1959 by the congregation of the Assembly of God Church, the building was the center for church activities until 1982, when it was sold and partly converted into a commercial kitchen.

The building was resold in 1986, and given a face lift in 1987 along with landscaping and interior modifications, which brought it more in line with the prevailing Victorian theme. The building was thus transformed into a business "incubator" for fledging small businesses. Five businesses now share the facilities:

NOTOCO - (makers of Earscopes) _____ Lew Nash, Jan Vogle, Vivian Olivera, Peggy Richardson, Arabelle & Paul Mueller
Kaytis Advertising & Secretarial Services _____ Nancy Kaytis, Lisa Sedam
Professional Hunter Supplies _____ Bill McBride, Andrea Jordan
Leonard D. Schappert, Certified Patent Attorney_ Leonard D. and Toni Schappert
JA'AMS Catering Service_____ Jae Boynton; Pam Anderson

Print # 1065
Sponsor: Lew Nash

Print # 1066
Sponsor: The Gotcher Family

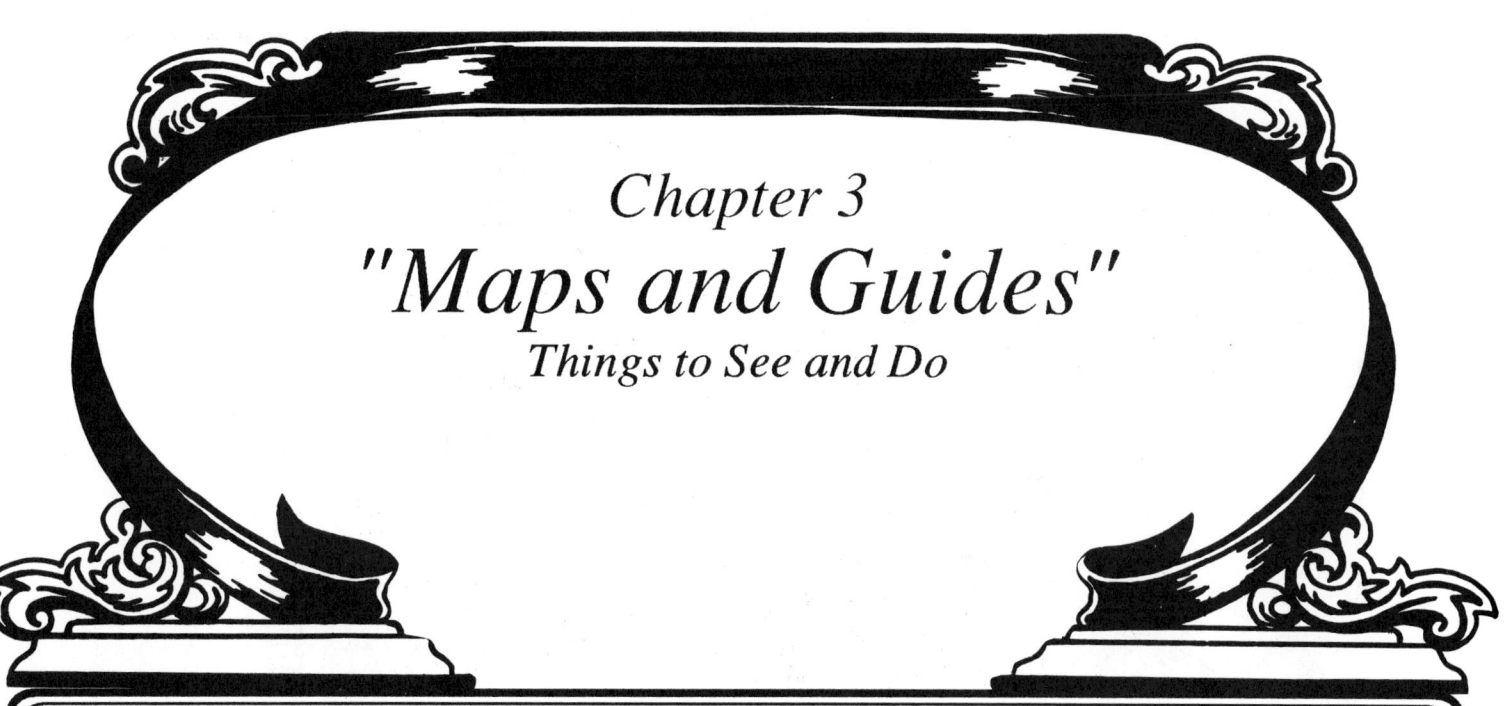

Chapter 3
"Maps and Guides"
Things to See and Do

	Print Number	Page
Map - City of Ferndale		68 & 69
Map - Ferndale & Vicinity		70
Business Listings/Directory		72
GUIDE: Things to See and Do		76
Fern Cottage	1078	78
Linden Hall	1079	79
Cliff's Village Carriage	1089	80
Parade	1081	81
February: Fireman's Games	1082	82
May: Celebration of the Holy Ghost	1083	83
May: Kinetic Sculpture Race		84 & 85
June: Mid Summer Festival	1086	86 & 87
July: 4th Parade	1088	88
December: Christmas in Ferndale	1089	89

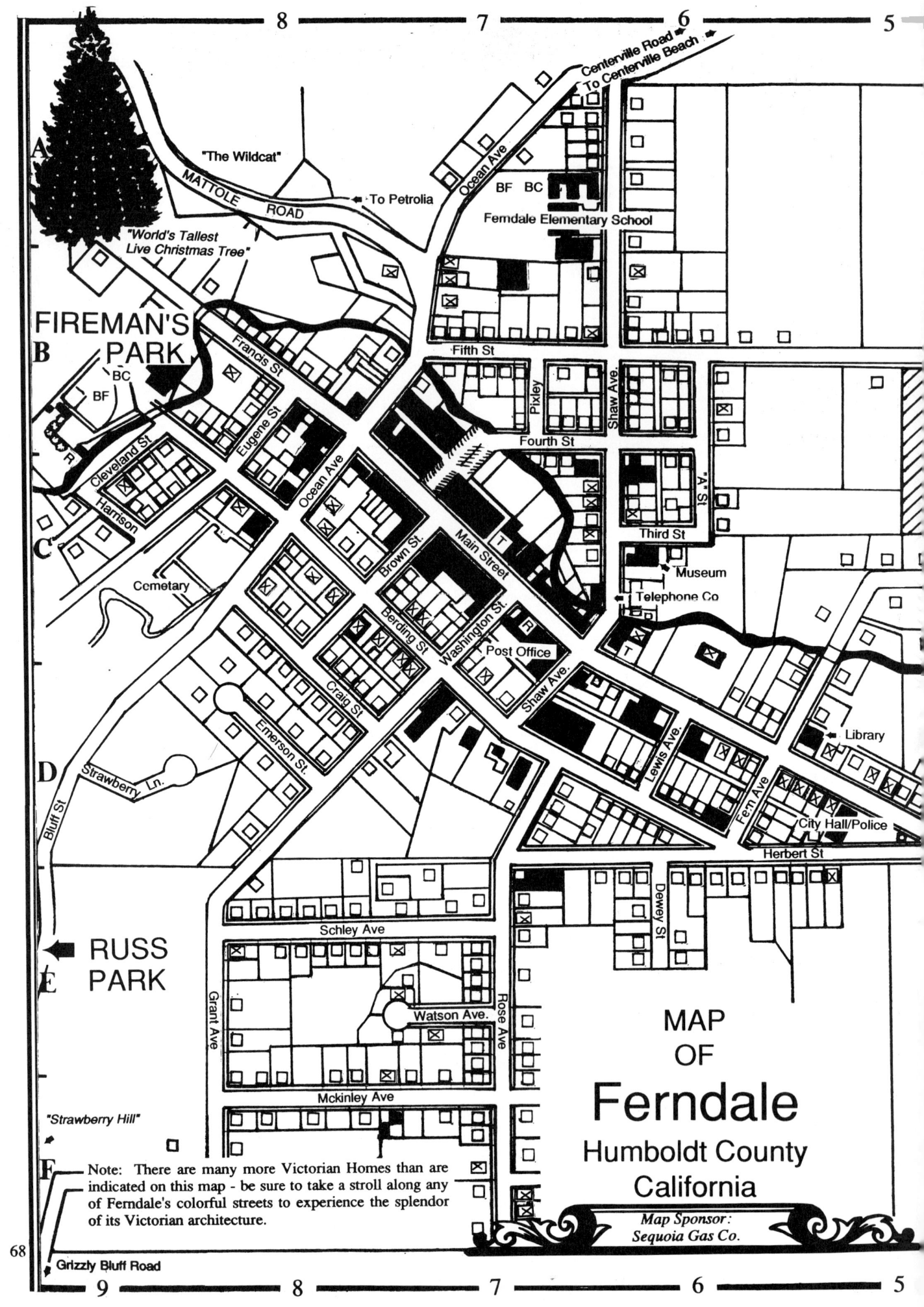

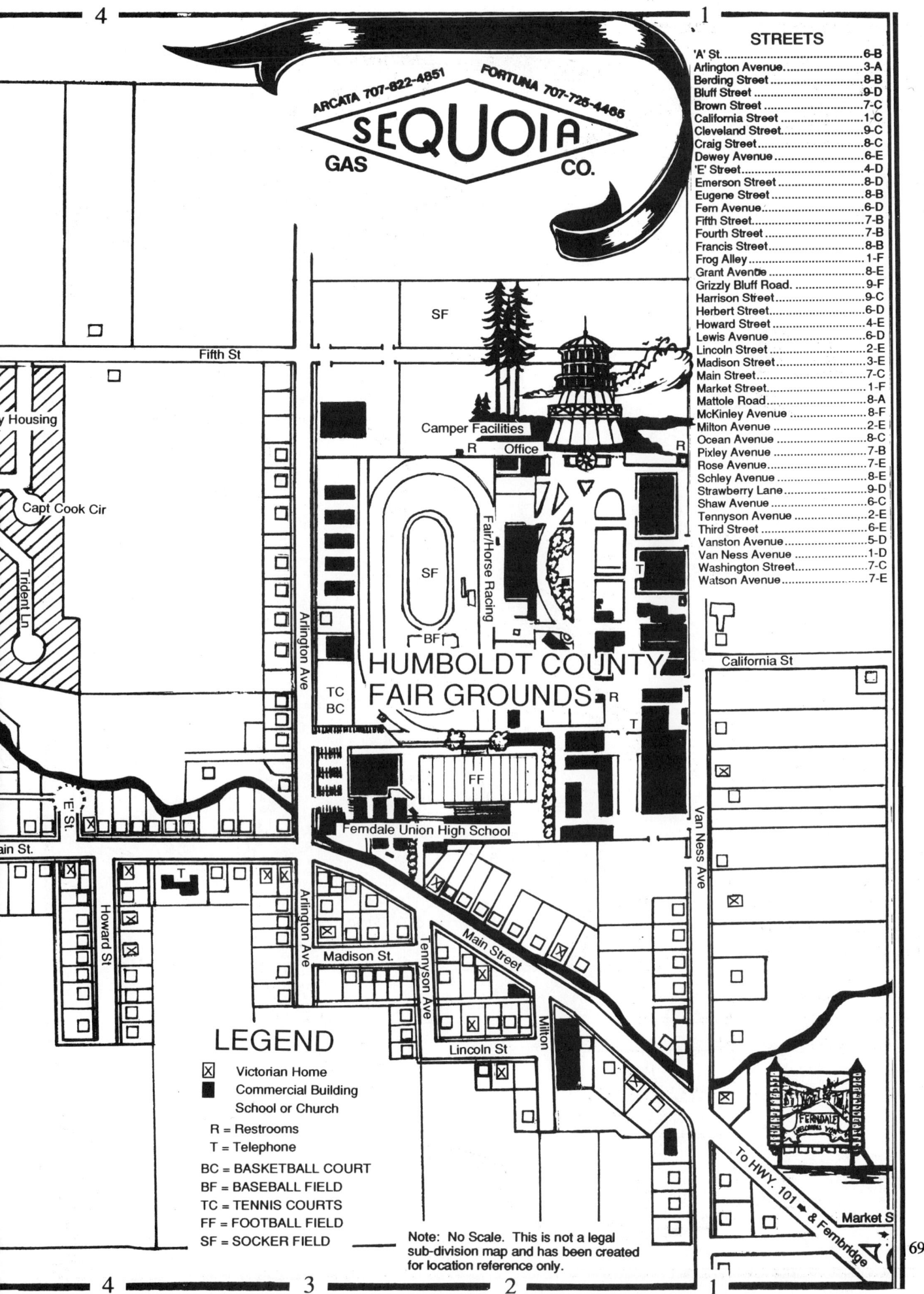

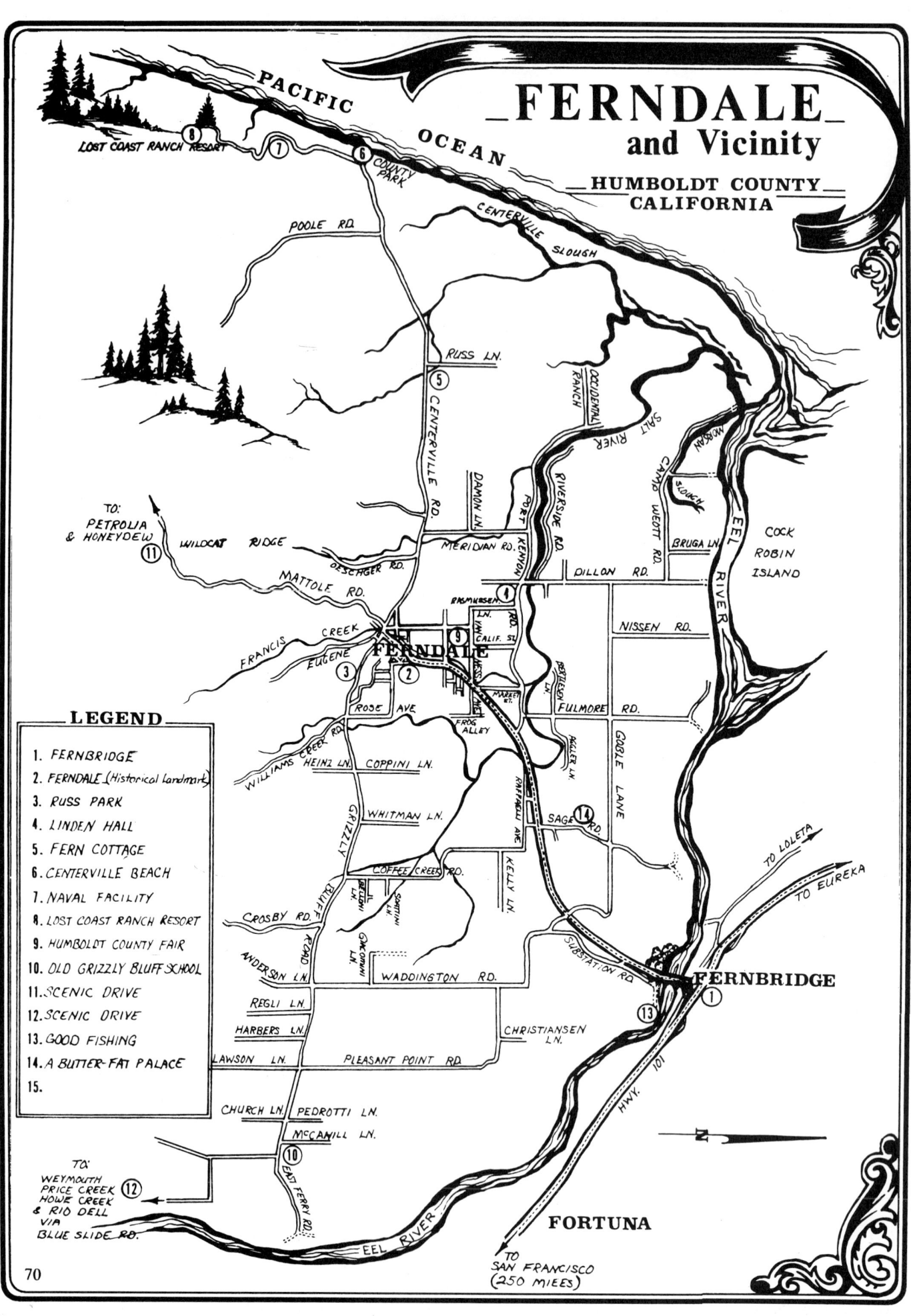

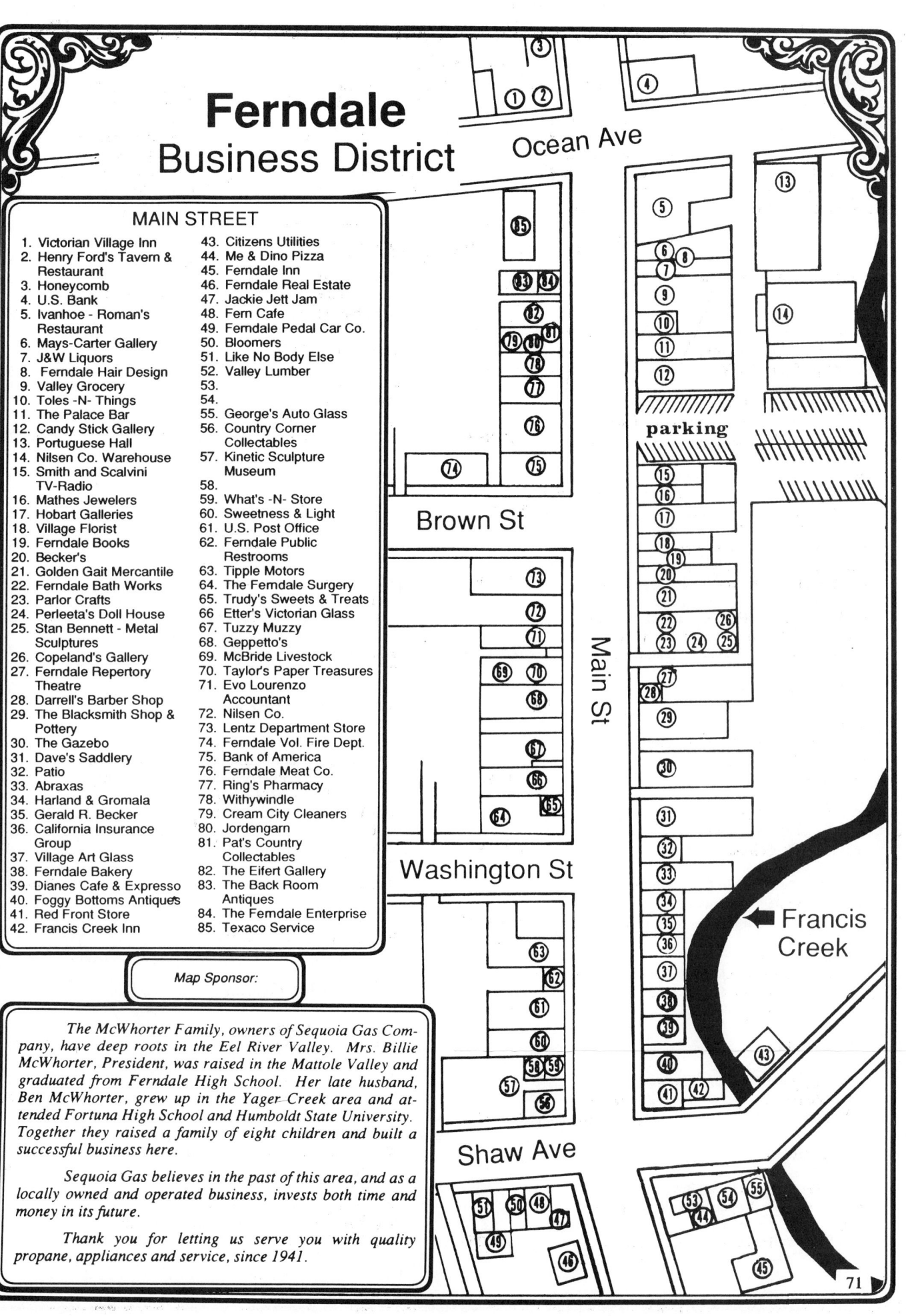

Ferndale
Business District

MAIN STREET

1. Victorian Village Inn
2. Henry Ford's Tavern & Restaurant
3. Honeycomb
4. U.S. Bank
5. Ivanhoe - Roman's Restaurant
6. Mays-Carter Gallery
7. J&W Liquors
8. Ferndale Hair Design
9. Valley Grocery
10. Toles -N- Things
11. The Palace Bar
12. Candy Stick Gallery
13. Portuguese Hall
14. Nilsen Co. Warehouse
15. Smith and Scalvini TV-Radio
16. Mathes Jewelers
17. Hobart Galleries
18. Village Florist
19. Ferndale Books
20. Becker's
21. Golden Gait Mercantile
22. Ferndale Bath Works
23. Parlor Crafts
24. Perleeta's Doll House
25. Stan Bennett - Metal Sculptures
26. Copeland's Gallery
27. Ferndale Repertory Theatre
28. Darrell's Barber Shop
29. The Blacksmith Shop & Pottery
30. The Gazebo
31. Dave's Saddlery
32. Patio
33. Abraxas
34. Harland & Gromala
35. Gerald R. Becker
36. California Insurance Group
37. Village Art Glass
38. Ferndale Bakery
39. Dianes Cafe & Expresso
40. Foggy Bottoms Antiques
41. Red Front Store
42. Francis Creek Inn
43. Citizens Utilities
44. Me & Dino Pizza
45. Ferndale Inn
46. Ferndale Real Estate
47. Jackie Jett Jam
48. Fern Cafe
49. Ferndale Pedal Car Co.
50. Bloomers
51. Like No Body Else
52. Valley Lumber
53.
54.
55. George's Auto Glass
56. Country Corner Collectables
57. Kinetic Sculpture Museum
58.
59. What's -N- Store
60. Sweetness & Light
61. U.S. Post Office
62. Ferndale Public Restrooms
63. Tipple Motors
64. The Ferndale Surgery
65. Trudy's Sweets & Treats
66. Etter's Victorian Glass
67. Tuzzy Muzzy
68. Geppetto's
69. McBride Livestock
70. Taylor's Paper Treasures
71. Evo Lourenzo Accountant
72. Nilsen Co.
73. Lentz Department Store
74. Ferndale Vol. Fire Dept.
75. Bank of America
76. Ferndale Meat Co.
77. Ring's Pharmacy
78. Withywindle
79. Cream City Cleaners
80. Jordengarn
81. Pat's Country Collectables
82. The Eifert Gallery
83. The Back Room Antiques
84. The Ferndale Enterprise
85. Texaco Service

Map Sponsor:

The McWhorter Family, owners of Sequoia Gas Company, have deep roots in the Eel River Valley. Mrs. Billie McWhorter, President, was raised in the Mattole Valley and graduated from Ferndale High School. Her late husband, Ben McWhorter, grew up in the Yager Creek area and attended Fortuna High School and Humboldt State University. Together they raised a family of eight children and built a successful business here.

Sequoia Gas believes in the past of this area, and as a locally owned and operated business, invests both time and money in its future.

Thank you for letting us serve you with quality propane, appliances and service, since 1941.

— Categories —

1. Antiques/Furniture
2. Art Galleries
3. Attorneys
4. Auto Repair
5. Banks
6. Beauty Shops
7. Bed & Breakfast Inns
8. Books/Magazines
9. Candy & Icecream
10. Churches
11. Clothing/Apparel
12. Cocktails
13. Doctors/Veterinarians
14. EMERGENCIES
15. Florist
16. Gifts & Novelties
17. Groceries/Liquor
18. Hardware - TV - radio
19. Jewelry
20. Laundry/Laundromat
21. Pharmacy
22. Real Estate
23. Recreation
24. Restaurants
25. Restrooms (Public)
26. Saddlery/Tack
27. Services
28. Signs/Commercial Art
29. Sporting Goods
30. Telephones (Public)
31. Video Rentals
32. Yardage & Notions

Business Listings/Directory:

1. **ANTIQUES/FURNITURE**

    #21 Golden Gait Mercantile
    A store from the past with something for everyone, including antique furniture.
    421 Main St, Ferndale..............................786-4891

    #24 Perleeta's Doll House
    Old dolls, vintage clothing, collectibles.
    427 Main St, Ferndale..............................786-9006

    #40 Foggy Bottoms Antiques
    Jewelry, porcelain, glass, furniture & collectibles.
    563 Main St, Ferndale..............................786-9300

    #92 Carriage House Antiques
    Furniture & Collectibles.
    606 Berding St, Ferndale 786-4086

    #135 Watkins & Frazier Cabinet & Furniture
    Cabinets and Custom furniture. Made to order.
    246 Berding St, Ferndale 786-4808

2. **ART GALLERIES**

    #12 Candy Stick Gallery
    Art Gallery & Hand-crafted jewelry from around the world.
    361 Main St, Ferndale 786-4600

    #17 Hobart Gallery
    Gallery of paintings, pottery, and sculpture.
    393 Main St, Ferndale................................725-3851

    #25 Stan Bennett Motion Sculpture
    Wire sculptures with motion.
    427 Main St, Ferndale................................786-4798

    #82 Eifert Gallery
    The wildlife and wilderness of the pacific Northwest.
    Larry Eifert • Carrie Grant. Open Daily.
    344 Main St, Ferndale................................786-4726

3. **ATTORNEYS**

    #94 Gerry McGee, Attorney at law.
    Specializing in litigation and trial practice.
     924 Fifth St, Eureka...............................443-6711

4. **AUTO REPAIR**

    #111 Ferndale Body & Glass
    Complete Body Repair & Auto Glass.
    Call: Chuck Morgan
    638 Main St, Ferndale................................786-9250

    #113 Ferndale Motors
    Auto Repair, towing. If it's mechanical we'll repair it.
    638 Main St, Ferndale.............................. 786-9526

5. **BEAUTY SHOPS**

    #3   Honeycomb
    The Family Hair Design Center.
    Owner: Rosemarie Hauger
    250 Francis St, Ferndale 786-4766

6. **BANKS**

    #75 Bank of America
    Checking and Savings ....(800) 523-3259
    394 Main St, Ferndale..............................786-9522

    #4   US Bank - Bank of Loleta
    You make the difference to us!
    Main & Ocean Streets, Ferndale............................ 786-9507

7. **BED & BREAKFAST INNS**
    See GUIDE: Page 117.

8. **BOOKS/MAGAZINES**

    #19 Ferndale Books
    Antiquarian, Out of print books, specializing in Travel, History, Poetry, California, Americana.
    Owners: Carlos & Marilyn Benemann
    405 Main St, PO Box 1034, Ferndale 786-9135

    #68 Geppetto's
    Books & Cards.
    452 Main St, Ferndale.............................. 786-4432

    #41 Red Front Store
    Magazines & paper supplies.
    577 Main St, Ferndale.............................. 786-9611

9. **CANDY & ICE CREAM**

    #9   Valley Grocery
    339 Main St, Ferndale.............................. 786-9515

    #41 Red Front Store
    577 Main St, Ferndale.............................. 786-9611

    #60 Sweetness & Light
    Traditional Chocolates & Candies.
    554 Main St, Ferndale.............................. 786-4403

    #65 Trudy's Sweets & Treats
    Bon Boniere Ice Cream & candy for kids.
    Main St, Ferndale

10. CHURCHES

#90 Church of the Assumption
Masses: Sat. 5:15 pm Sun. 8:30 am & 10:30 am
546 Berding St, Ferndale 786-9551

#112 First Congregational Church of Ferndale
Independant-Evangelical Rev. David Kilmer
Sunday - Worship Services 10:30 am
Sunday School - 11:00 am
Tuesday Bible study/prayer - 7:30 pm
712 Main St, Ferndale................................ 786-4475

#106 Our Saviors Lutheran Church E.L.C.A.
4th & Shaw Ave, Ferndale.......................... 786-9619

#114 St. Marks Lutheran L.C.M.S.
795 Berding St, Ferndale

#131 Ferndale Foursquare Church
Ferndale 786-9118

11. CLOTHING/APPAREL

#31. Dave's Saddlery
Western wear, boots, hats, jeans, and
outwear for the entire family.
491 Main St, Ferndale................................786-4004

#59 What's 'N' Store
Active wear and more.
580 Main St, Ferndale................................ 786-9660

#80 Jordengarn
The Finest in Natural Fiber. Custom handknits,
natural fiber yarn. Not your usual women's apparel.
350 Main St, Ferndale................................786-4111

#73 Lentz Dept. Store
Fashions for women, men, and children,
also yardage and notions.
Main & Brown St, Ferndale........................786-4644

#50 Bloomers
Custom sewing, clothing design, and alterations.
Located in the Shaw Building.
620 Shaw Ave, Ferndale............................786-9064

12. COCKTAILS

#2 Henry Fords Tavern (Victorian Village Inn)
Ocean Ave, Ferndale 786-9400

#11 The Palace
353 Main St, Ferndale................................786-4165

#129 Angelina Inn
281 Fernbridge Dr, Fortuna, CA..................725-3153

13. DOCTORS/DENTISTS/VETERINARIANS

#64 The Ferndale Surgery & Family Care
Ray Wiser, MD - Robin Smith F.N.P.,
492 Main St, P.O. Box 1208, Ferndale.................. 786-4028

#91 Valley Veterinary
Joseph Humble D.V.M., M.P.V.M.
600 Berding, Ferndale 786-9229

#121 Ferndale Veterinary
Charles Ozanian D.V.M.
1140 Van Ness, Ferndale 786-4200

14. EMERGENCIES

Medical Emergency 911
Fire 786-4114
Ambulance 725-5179
Police.. 786-4225
Sheriff ....(1) 445-7251
Hospital 725-3361
Redwood Memorial, 3300 Renner Dr, Fortuna

15. FLORIST

#18 Village Florist
Flowers for every occasion. Balloons and gift items.
399 Main St, Ferndale............................. 786-9748

16. GIFTS & NOVELTIES

#10 Toles 'n' Things
Redwood gift items, wood & folk art supplies,
tole painting classes.
341 Main St, Ferndale............................ 786-4084

#12 Candy Stick Gallery
Arts & handcrafted jewelry.
361 Main St, Ferndale............................ 786-4600

#16 Mathes Jewelry
389 Main St, Ferndale............................ 786-4641

#17 Hobart Gallery
393 Main St, Ferndale............................ 725-3851

#18 Village Florist
399 Main St, Ferndale............................ 786-9748

#21 Golden Gait Mercantile
421 Main St, Ferndale............................ 786-4891

#22 Ferndale Bath Works
Personal care bath, beauty, & gift shop
with soaps & custom scents.
425 Main St, Ferndale............................ 786-9494

#23 Parlor Crafts
Needlecrafts, cross stitch, quilting, fabrics,
craft books, and supplies.
431 Main St, Ferndale............................ 786-9572

#25 Stan Bennett Metal Sculptures
Marble machines & sculptures.
427 Main St, Ferndale............................ 786-4798

#26 G. Copeland Design Studio
Wearable art, gift boutique, on the boardwalk
425 Main St, (hall shops), Ferndale 786-9083

#30 The Gazebo
American Folk Art and Furniture, Scandinavian and English
Crafts. Paul, Suzannah and Paige Mellon.
475 Main St, Ferndale............................ 786-9853

#33 Abraxas Leather Shop
505 Main St, Ferndale.. 786-1288

#37 Village Art Glass
Custom stained & leaded glass windows, original custom designs, lamps & repair. Also: Member of Stained Glass Association of America.
535 Main St, Ferndale.. 786-4318

#47 Jackie Jett Jam
Using the best Northcoast berries and fruits Jackie Jett prepares her "homemade" jams in 6 to 10 cup batches. The flavor is incomparable. A full spectrum of taste sensations is available in 15 varieties of jam. Shipped USA in attractive gift box. Brochure on request.
606 Main St, Ferndale.. 786-4729

#67 Tuzzy Muzzy Gifts
468 Main St, Ferndale.. 786-9857

#68 Geppetto's
Nostalgic toys, cards, and gifts. Owner: Gwen Roberts.
452 Main St, Ferndale.. 786-4432

#72 Nilsen Co.
General store and hardware.
424 Main St, Ferndale.. 786-9501

#77 Rings Pharmacy
Cards, Gifts, and novelties.
362 Main St, Ferndale.. 786-4511

#78 Withywindle
Handcrafted stoneware, porcelain, jewelry, glass, wearable art & woods.
358 Main St, Ferndale.. 786-9610

17. GROCERIES/LIQUOR

#9 Valley Grocery
Fresh meats and produce, complete grocery store.
8 am - 6 pm Monday - Saturday.
339 Main St, Ferndale.. 786-9515

#41 Red Front Store
Beer, wine, & miscellaneous groceries.
577 Main St, Ferndale.. 786-9611

#76 Ferndale Meat Co.
Choice meats, custom cutting and wrapping, old fashioned sugar curing & smoking, Ranch butchering, frozen food storage lockers.
376 Main St, Ferndale.. 786-4501

#119 Lorenzo's Gas & Grocery
Milton and Main, Ferndale 786-4503

#126 Nobles Grocery (& gas)
Open Daily 8 - 8; Sunday 10 - 6.
Arlynda, Ferndale 786-4252

18. HARDWARE - TV/RADIO

#15 Smith and Scalvini
TV's, auto radio & stereo systems. Hi-fi and stereo, antennas, satellite dealer, and video recorders.
385 Main St, Ferndale.. 786-4575

#72 Nilsen Company
Hardware & general store.
424 Main St, Ferndale.. 786-9501

19. JEWELRY

#12 Candy Stick Gallery
Hand crafted jewelry.
361 Main St, Ferndale.. 786-4600

#16 Mathes Jewelers
Fine traditional jewelry. Excellence in watch and clock repair.
389 Main St, Ferndale.. 786-4641

#26 G. Copeland Design Studio
Wearable Art & Designer Jewelry. On the Boardwalk.
425 Main St, (hall shops), Ferndale 786-9083

#33 Abraxas Leather Shop
Jewelry, fine leather, pottery, glass, figurines, & crafts.
505 Main St, Ferndale.. 786-1288

#59 What's N' Store
580 Main St, Ferndale.. 786-9660

#73 Lentz Department Store
Main & Brown St, Ferndale.................................. 786-4644

#78 Withywindle
Jewelry & Wearable Art.
358 Main St, Ferndale.. 786-9610

20. LAUNDRY

#109 Ferndale Laudromat
Drop Service-Self Service. Fuller Brush Products.
Proprietors: Sanford & Dorian Lowry.
632 Main St, Ferndale.. 786-9471

21. PHARMACY

#77 Rings Pharmacy
362 Main St, Ferndale.. 786-4511

22. REAL ESTATE

#130 Ferndale Real Estate
Homes, Commercial & Ranches.
Member of Multiple Listing.
614 Main St, Ferndale.. 786-4651

23. RECREATION
See GUIDE ... page 75.

#27 Ferndale Repertory Theatre
Theatrical Entertainment.
447 Main St, Ferndale.. 725-2378

#49 Ferndale Pedal Car Co.
People powered horseless carriages and bikes. Hourly Rentals.
606 Main St, Ferndale

#122 Cliff's Village Carriage
Horse drawn carriage for special occasions by advanced reservation.
Call Cliff: 786-4042

24. RESTAURANTS/SNACKS
See GUIDE ... page 108.

25. RESTROOMS (public)

#62 Ferndale Public Restrooms
Next to Post Office, Main St.

#100 Fireman's Park

#124 Humboldt County Fair Grounds

26. SADDLERY/TACK

#31 Dave's Saddlery
Saddles, tack and supplies.
491 Main St., Ferndale............................786-4004

#72 Nilsen Company
Tack & supplies
424 Main Street, Ferndale........................786-9501

27. SERVICES

#36 California Insurance Group
Northcoast Branch. Serving Ferndale and Humboldt
County since 1898.
523 Main St, Ferndale............................786-4023

#50 Bloomers
Custom Sewing, clothing design and alterations.
Located in the Shaw Building.
620 Shaw Ave, Ferndale..........................786-9064

#66 Etter's Victorian Glass
Custom Picture Framing and Antique Furniture
Restoration.
476 Main St, Ferndale

#71 Evo Lourenzo Accountant
Accountant, Notory Public, Enrolled
Agent for Income Tax.
430 Main St, Ferndale............................786-4222

#93 Kaytis Advertising & Secretarial Services
Printing, typesetting, business cards, labels, stationery,
brochures, flyers, menus, programs, invitations, General
typing, leases, resumes, FAX, self-service copies
660 Berding St., Ferndale 786-4904

Avon Representative - Marlene S. True
490 Shaw, Ferndale 786-9347

#93 Notoco
Makers of Earscopes, Lew Nash.
660 Berding, Ferndale 786-4400

#110 Northcoast Pumphouse
We sell the Best & Service the rest.
Owner: Don Laffranchi.
132 Main St, Ferndale 786-4281

#22 Ferndale Bath Works
Custom Fragrance Center
425 Main St, Ferndale............................ 786-9494

#125 Doug's Refrigeration
Dairy services and supplies.
989 Milton Ave, Ferndale........................786-4294

#136 Sequoia Gas
Propane tanks, piping, sales & service.
926 Main St, Fortuna..............................725-4465

Toste Construction
Building Restoration, remodeling and new construction.
License #547197....................................786-4813

28. SIGNS/COMMERCIAL ART

#123 Carriage House Studio
Custom Redwood Signs, Etched Glass, and Artwork
SANDBLASTING Commercial or Personal.
Call: Cliff & Donna Setterlund, Ferndale........786-4042

29. SPORTING GOODS

#41 Red Front Sporting Goods
577 Main St, Ferndale............................786-9611

Fernbridge Market
Fernbridge, CA 725-3852

30. TELEPHONES (public)

#43 Citizen's Utilities of California
550 Shaw St, Ferndale
Business Office 786-9544
TDD-TTY only 786-9070
Repair Service 611

PUBLIC TELEPHONE LOCATIONS
C.U.C.C. (Telephone office) .... 550 Shaw
George's Glass.................................. 607 Main
Ferndale Repertory............................. 447 Main
Veteran's Building.............................. 1100 Main
Ferndale High Gym .... 1231 Main
Belotti Hall .... Fairgrounds
Sheep Barn .... Fairgrounds

31. VIDEO RENTALS

#7 J&W Liquors
337 Main St, Ferndale............................786-4555

#41 Red Front Store
577 Main St, Ferndale............................786-9611

#126 Nobles Grocery
Arlynda, Ferndale 786-4252

32. YARDAGE & NOTIONS

#40 Parlor Crafts
Needlepoint fabrics, craft supplies and craftbooks.
431 Main St, Ferndale............................786-9572

#73 Lentz Department Store
Large selection of yardage, notions and craft supplies. Main
& Brown St, Ferndale 786-4644

GUIDE: "Things to See & Do"

*February - **Fireman's Games** ... page 82.*

*March - **Foggy Bottoms Milk Run***
    A family affair of 3 different running courses through Ferndale farmlands to the finish on Main Street.

*May - **Craft Fair***
    Northcoast crafts people display and sell their wares during the annual event at Portuguese Hall.

*May - **Holy Ghost Festival***
    The Portuguese people of the area celebrate with parades, dances, meals and an auction. An annual Ferndale event ... page 83

*May - **Bicycle Tour of the Unknown Coast***
    A bike race & tour beginning and ending in Ferndale.

*May - **The Great Arcata to Ferndale Cross-Country Kinetic Sculpture Race***
    Takes place over land and water for 3 days and 2 nights ending in Ferndale. Attracts wild and crazy people-powered contraptions from across the nation, to race for the glory! ... page 84 & 85.

*May - **Memorial Day Parade***
    Ferndale Veterans parade down Main Street.

*June - **Mid-Summer Scandinavian Festival***
    Parades, music, food, dances, events, and costumes. A two day festival ... page 86&87

*July - **July 4th Parade***
    Henry Ford's Tavern, Invitational Antique Ford Rally and Parade ... page 88

Other Things to See & Do

#99 Russ Park ... A true wilderness park with trails leading to a pond and views overlooking the Eel Valley. There are trails that may be used as footpaths, also trails for horseback riding. No wheeled vehicles allowed so wear good walking shoes. Park located one-half mile east of Protestant Cemetary on Bluff Road.

#98 Fireman's Park ... Public recreation area including picnic grounds, barbecue pits, playground, athletic field, and basketball courts. Located at the south end of Berding Street.

Protestant & Catholic Cemeteries ... Don't miss a walk through our cemeteries. The beauty of the old monuments and stair stepped plots are to be enjoyed by all. The peacefulness that holds our past offers those who come to share it a moment when time stands still. You will see their names and in some small way help their memories live on. ... page 30

Centerville Beach County Park ... Easy access to beach for excellent walking and sight seeing. Watch for whales. Five miles west of Ferndale on Centerville Beach Road (narrow winding road).

Wildlife and Bird Watching ... Excellent variety of animals, water fowl and bird life around the entire area. Please respect private property and safety rules. A Wildlife Guide to the Eel River Delta is available at the Eifert Gallery.

Wildcat Road ... A mountainous road that journeys up Ferndale's backdrop. Many panoramic views, but use caution for the roads are dangerous. Take a 3 hour afternoon drive through Petrolia then back to 101 South.

Fishing ... Eel River - Early season trout and late summer half-pounders to the most exciting of them all, salmon and steelhead.

Ocean fishing - from the beaches or by way of sports fishing docks on nearby Humboldt Bay. Also, Razorback clams, Humboldt crabs, and other shell fish can be taken in season.

#107 Ferndale Museum ... Ferndale's latest institution is it's museum. A product of hard work, sweat and laughter, the museum is a repository for farm wagons and settees, cream separators and valentines, old bottles and a Bosch-Omoriseismograph, sensitive to earthquakes all over the world. The museum is also a living history classroom with rotating exhibits. We welcome you to see our past and enjoy our treasures.

Yearly Activities And Events

August - **Humboldt County Fair**
   The Fair features rides, food, attractions, games, livestock, horse racing and unique opportunities. It's not the biggest fair in the state, but what the Humboldt County Fair lacks in size it makes up for in down-home family fun. As in past years, horseracing will again be the main attraction—always at the Humboldt County Fairgrounds.

September - **Antique Show**
   Sponsored by the Ferndale Museum with dealers from far & wide.

October - **Theatre**
   The Season's opening production.

November - **Blue Grass Festival**
   Produced by Bill Fales - held at the theatre.

November - **Christmas Craft Sale**
   Gifts and goodies to start off the holiday season.

December - **Christmas Tree Lighting**
   A celebration of Christmas with a ceremony and the lighting of the World's Tallest Living Christmas Tree. The streets of Ferndale are lined with small trees and decorations leading up to the splendor of the big tree. Ferndale's Volunteer Fire Department spends weeks in preparation for the moment of the lighting when the Christmas season is officially started. The tree, seen for miles around, is a proud tradition of our community ... page 89.

For more information on the above events and festivities, please write or call our Chamber of Commerce, P.O. Box 325, Ferndale, CA 95536-0325; (707) 786-4477

Other Things to See & Do

#27 Ferndale Repertory Theatre ... The Ferndale Repertory Theatre was established in 1971 to bring high quality live theatrical entertainment to the residents and visitors of Humboldt County. Originally an all volunteer organization, the Rep has grown to be a professionally directed, year round production company offering the best in comedies, dramas, fantasies and musicals. The theatre operates out of the Village Playhouse, built in 1920, and has established a reputation statewide for unique and highly entertaining productions and was recognized as "one of the best rural theatres in California" by the California Arts Council in 1988. For an experience to make your visit to Ferndale complete, don't miss a performance. P.O. Box 892, Ferndale, CA 95536 (707) 725-2378

Camp Weott Guide Service ... Tour the river channels and salt marshes where the Eel River meets the sea. For reservations call Bruce Slocum 786-4187 8:30 - 10 a.m. RFD Box 248, Ferndale. Brochure on request

Cliff's Village Carriage ... Available for Weddings and special occasions by advanced reservation (April through Sept., locally) Call: Cliff Setterlund 786-4042 P.O. Box 712, Ferndale, CA 95536 ... page 80.

Ferndale Pedal Car Co... Featuring people-powered horseless carriages. Hourly rentals to tour our Victorian Village at a pace you can enjoy. 786-9417 Main St, Ferndale, CA 95536

Golden Gait Mercantile Museum... Free museum on the 2nd floor complete with Toy Store, General store, Hat Shop and Antiques. 421 Main St, Ferndale, 786-4891 ... pages 44 & 45

Kinetic Sculpture Museum ... Located in the Peers Building. A collection of Kinetic Sculptures from past years. Some of them are still being used. 580 Main St, Ferndale ... pages 84 & 85

Ferndale Historical Homes Open for Tours Nestled against the hills surrounding the Eel River Valley the village of Ferndale, with it's wealth of Victorian homes and architecture, has survived the changes of time, and today has become a popular West Coast attraction. Two of the areas historic homes, Fern Cottage and Linden Hall are open to the public and offer an exciting glimpse into early day life in the Eel River Valley. Please call for days and times. Linden Hall 786-4908 Fern Cottage 786-4835 or 786-4735 (large tours by advanced appointment) ... pages 78 & 79

"Fern Cottage" Russ Family Home

Nestled against the hills surrounding the Eel River Valley, the village of Ferndale, with it's wealth of Victorian homes and architecture has survived the changes of time, and has now become a popular West Coast attraction. Two of the area historic homes, Fern Cottage and Linden Hall (next page) are open to the public and offer an exciting glimpse into early day life in the Eel River Valley.

Fern Cottage was first an eight room farm house with a wide veranda across the front. The original land patent was issued to Joseph Russ in 1866; the house was built the same year. Several additions were made in the last quarter of the nineteenth century. The site was chosen by Joseph's wife Zipporah. Fern Cottage and the surrounding ranch are still owned by their descendants.

Fern Cottage is a picturesque 19th century settlement farmhouse, the home of a large and extended family-run ranching operation of dairies, sheep and cattle. Retaining a high degree of architectural and historic integrity, Fern Cottage is significant for its simple, gracious architecture which has been carefully preserved. Fern Cottage has been named to the National Register of Historic Places. Its physical and historic character has been reserved so completely that its roots have remained clear and enduring. Through more than half a century, the fabric and content of the house has changed little.

Fern cottage is a non-profit foundation.
Please call for days and times
Linden hall (707) 786-4908
Fern Cottage (707) 786-4835 or 786-4735
Large Tours by advance appointment

Print #1078
Sponsor: Fern Cottage

"Linden Hall"
The F. W. Andreasen Home

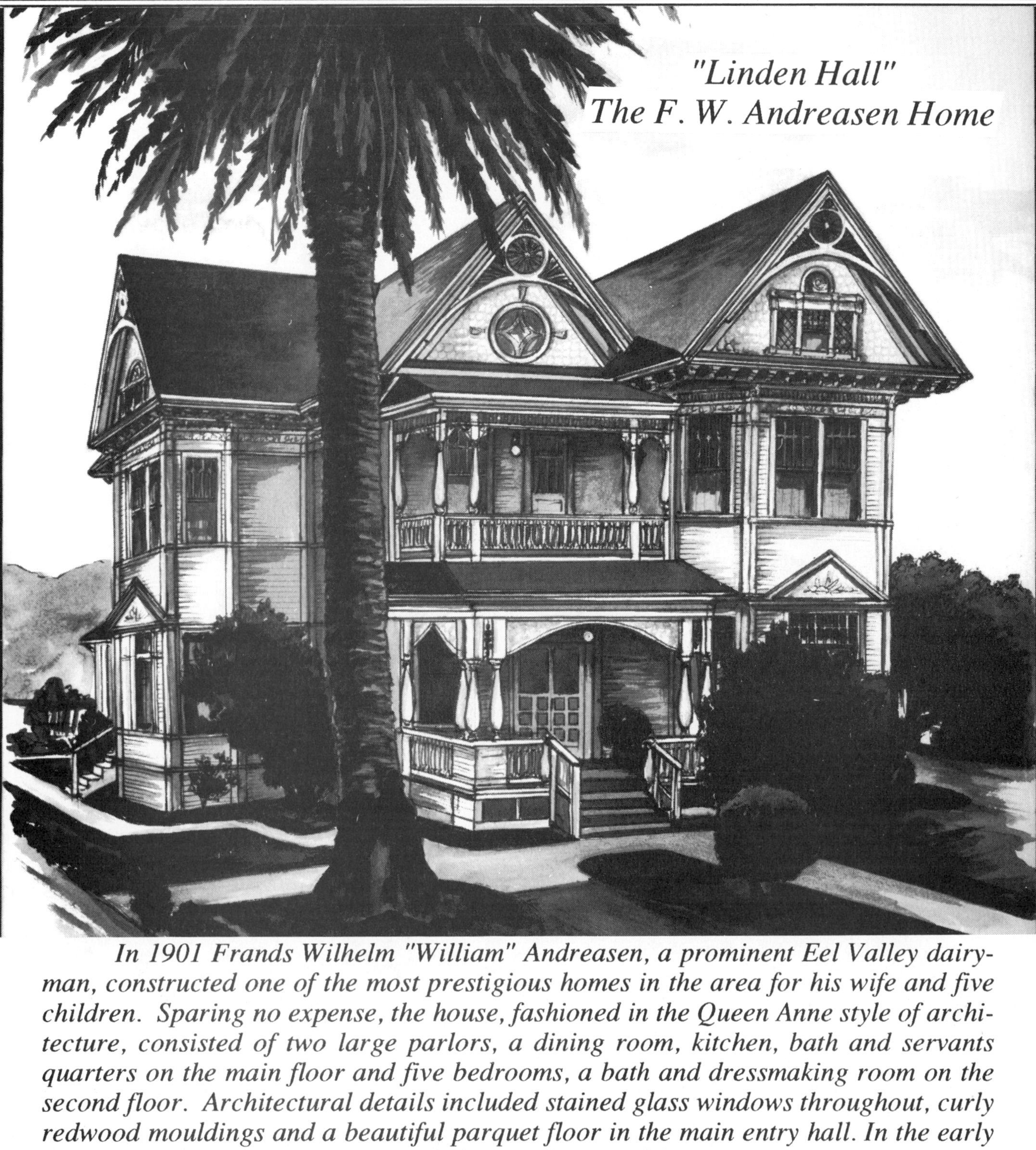

In 1901 Frands Wilhelm "William" Andreasen, a prominent Eel Valley dairyman, constructed one of the most prestigious homes in the area for his wife and five children. Sparing no expense, the house, fashioned in the Queen Anne style of architecture, consisted of two large parlors, a dining room, kitchen, bath and servants quarters on the main floor and five bedrooms, a bath and dressmaking room on the second floor. Architectural details included stained glass windows throughout, curly redwood mouldings and a beautiful parquet floor in the main entry hall. In the early days the house was known as the "Skim Milk House" because Andreasen picked up all the skim milk that wasn't used at the dairies to feed his pigs.

Most recently, Linden Hall (named for Mrs. Andreasen, whose maiden name was Lind) was nominated to the National Register of Historic Places, was restored and is now open for public viewing. The house contains many of its original furnishings, gas lighting fixtures and the original parlor wallpaper. Four of the twenty-four acres surrounding the house are being developed into an English Country Garden.

Print # 1079
Sponsor: Linden Hall

#122 "Cliff's Village Carriage"

Step back in time and enjoy a moment from the past. Our authentic 100 year old wicker carriage is available to a sellect few for weddings & special occasions. Cliff along with "Miss", the carriage horse, will proudly show you the sights.

Print # 1080
Sponsor: Cliff Setterlund

"Lots of Parades"

Our community may be small but the love in our hearts is big. We love to have parades and get everyone out to be a part of our celebrations. Whether it is Memorial Day, the 4th of July, or a Pet Parade, you will see our people come out to enjoy the festivities and share friendship and good times.

Print # 1081
Sponsor: Carriage House Studio

#74 "Firemen's Games"
Ferndale Volunteer Fire Dept

Every February our Ferndale Volunteer Fire Department comes out to show their stuff to the community as the four companies compete against eachother in the firemen's games. Using buckets, hoses and old time engines, several events can be seen. Our department also travels to other statewide events to compete. Although this is all great fun, we are, each and every one of us, proud of our fire department. All one has to do is be on Main Street when that fire alarm sounds, and watch our volunteers sprint out of their businesses, out of warehouses, out of the fields, and come running to the aid of their neighbors and friends. In only seconds, the first engine pulls out of the firehouse, volunteers hanging on, speeding away to the rescue. Yes, we are proud of them, and feel safer knowing they're there.

Print # 1082
Sponsor: Carriage House Studio

"The Celebration of the Holy Ghost"

The Holy Ghost Festival originated in Portugal in the 13th Century after Portugal had suffered a severe three year drought. When conditions did not improve, three sailing vessels were sent out to other countries to bring back food for the starving people.

One day, which was Whit or Pentecost Sunday, the dry grass and even the trees became inflamed from the terrible heat. The fire burned for three days. Children wept with hunger. Isabel, who was queen of Portugal, came down from her palace to walk among the children, and she and her attendants tried to console them. She removed her crown and placed it on the heads of the little girls to quiet them. She took the little children, the older people following, into the church to pray to the Holy Ghost.

After the service, the people came into the streets again and saw what they believed to be doves fly into the flames to extinguish them. Then they sighted the three tardy vessels coming into port with food.

A great feast was held, called the feast of the Holy Ghost. Late that night it started to rain. Variations have occured over the years, but the procession to the Church, the crowning of a child and a general celebration is a custom the Portuguese people brought to the United States and still celebrate in Ferndale today.

Print # 1083
Sponsor: Portuguese Association

Kinetic Sculpture Race

The first sculpture race was born in 1969 and began at Fields Landing. In 1976 the starting point was moved to Arcata. The race lasts three, long, grueling days: the first night the racers stay overnight in Eureka; the second day involves crossing the Humboldt Bay (with the Coast Guard hovering close by), only to look forward to an overnighter at the desolate "Camp Calistoga," on the beach; the third day the machines cross endless miles of sand and venture into the waves of the Eel River, then they move across farm lands through Port Kenyon to Ferndale and thus concludes this Glorious World Championship Arcata to Ferndale Cross Country Kinetic Sculpture Race, which is always held on Memorial Weekend.

The Kinetic Kops and "The Koppers Koop"

Some of the Kops have been involved with the race since one small pot of beans fed everyone. Having done everything in the race from coordinating to officiating, the Kinetic Kops are now the "Good Guys" and race right along side everyone else. Their official responsibility is to enforce rule #1000 which is a MANDATORY rule for all Sculpture Pilots, Pit Crew People, Officials, Spectators, Police, Sheriffs, Timers, and Passers-by to put great effort into HAVING FUN! For it is such craziness as this that keeps us all sane! The Koppers motto: "When in Doubt, SMILE!"

Calistoga Truck Story

This magnificent machine is an exact copy of the Calistoga Sparkling Water Company's first delivery truck. Well, it's slightly oversized, and we did take some artistic license with color. This beauty comes complete with an exotic "Hobatron" slip-clutch for SMOOTH acceleration. Aside from carrying a fire extinquisher, bucket, and toothbrushes, which are required, a "push" rope is kept on board. (In the event that a small boat might need help while crossing the Humboldt Bay.) Sixteen pilots power the overwhelming truck, fighting terrain, water and weather.

"Loppy Eared Loser"

Tyler Bramble (12 yrs) and Denise Crlenjak (13) were the youngest to complete the 1983 Kinetic Sculpture race, in their own creation the "Loppy Eared Loser".

Dale Olsen "Granpa" *from Ferndale California*

Born in downtown Ferndale, 63 year old Dale Olsen has made Ferndale his home most of his life. Dale is locally known as Granpa, which transpired from his active participation in the World Championship Kinetic Sculpture Race. 1989 marks a decade of racing for Dale, although he was pushing a sculpture that first year. A wild idea entered his mind the second year, and he built a machine with a six foot kite. It was called "Granpa's Flying Machine," hence came his local name. Unfortuneately, the wind was blowing the wrong direction, making travel very difficult. Four races later granpa perfected his machine, using a bicycle-like design. In his own words, "I have one now that will go all the way FOR THE GLORY!"

"The Danish Dance Team"

Print # 1086
Sponsor: Ady & Myrtle Setterlund

On the evening of February 6, 1951, a meeting of representatives of local Scandinavian lodges was held. The purpose of this get-together was to hold a Scandinavian festival. This first festival attracted a large turn-out and was a popular success.

"Scandinavian Midsummer Festival"
Velkommen til Forbindelsestad

Greetings and a hearty Velkommen to all on behalf of the Scandinavian Mid-Summer Festival Association. The Festival Association consists of all the Scandinavian Lodges, Danish, Finnish, Swedish, and Norwegian. Committees are chosen from the various lodges and all work together for one common purpose, "To promote the Heritage and Culture of Scandinavia." Every summer we enjoy the two day event in order to preserve our traditions and we encourage and display our knowledge of Scandinavian music, songs and dances. We celebrate with food, entertainment, native costume, flag ceremonies and dancing by the Danish adult and children's dance teams, then public dancing to Scandinavian music. Each year the festival is scheduled to take place in June. Try to be there!

Sponsor: Ferndale Danish Lodge

"Fourth of July Parade"

An invitational Antique Ford Rally and Parade sponsored by Henry Ford's Tavern can be enjoyed during a July Fourth visit to Ferndale.

Print # 1088
Sponsor: Victorian Village Inn

"Christmas in Ferndale"

Ferndale becomes a sparkling town of lights at Christmas time when Main Street is lined with small trees and decorations lead up to the splendor of the World's Tallest Living Christmas Tree. The whole community comes out to enjoy the ceremony as the season is officially started. The holiday season just wouldn't be the same without our big tree. The Ferndale Volunteer Fire Department spends weeks in preparation for the moment of the lighting. Carolers sing, cookies and hot chocolate are enjoyed and the lights come on wishing a Merry Christmas to all.

Print # 1089
Sponsor: Carriage House Studio

Chapter 4
"Meet our People"

*The people make the town.
Take a look at some of our people,
we're proud of them.*

—Index—

	Print Number	Page Number
Tony and Dorothy Lorenzo	7091	91
A Celebration of Life	1092	92
Evo Lourenzo	1093	93
Beckers Bench	1094	94
A Small Town Doctor "Wiser"	1095	95
Around town "Chris and Mary"		96
Around town "Trudy and John"		97
Four O'clock Coffee Club	1098	98
Friendly Faces	1099	99
Strong Roots	1100	100
Our Teachers "Fales & Mr. P"	1101	101
A Saddle Maker "Dave"	1102	102
Hobart	1103	103
Our Children	1104	104
A Friendly Welcome	1105	105
Volunteers on Call	1106	106

"Tony and Dorothy Lorenzo"

As a life-long resident of Ferndale, Tony has owned several local businesses including the Ivanhoe and the Palace. Now retired, he actively helps his wife Dorothy with "Ferndale Real Estate," their latest venture.

Print # 1091
Sponsor: Don and Michelle Smith

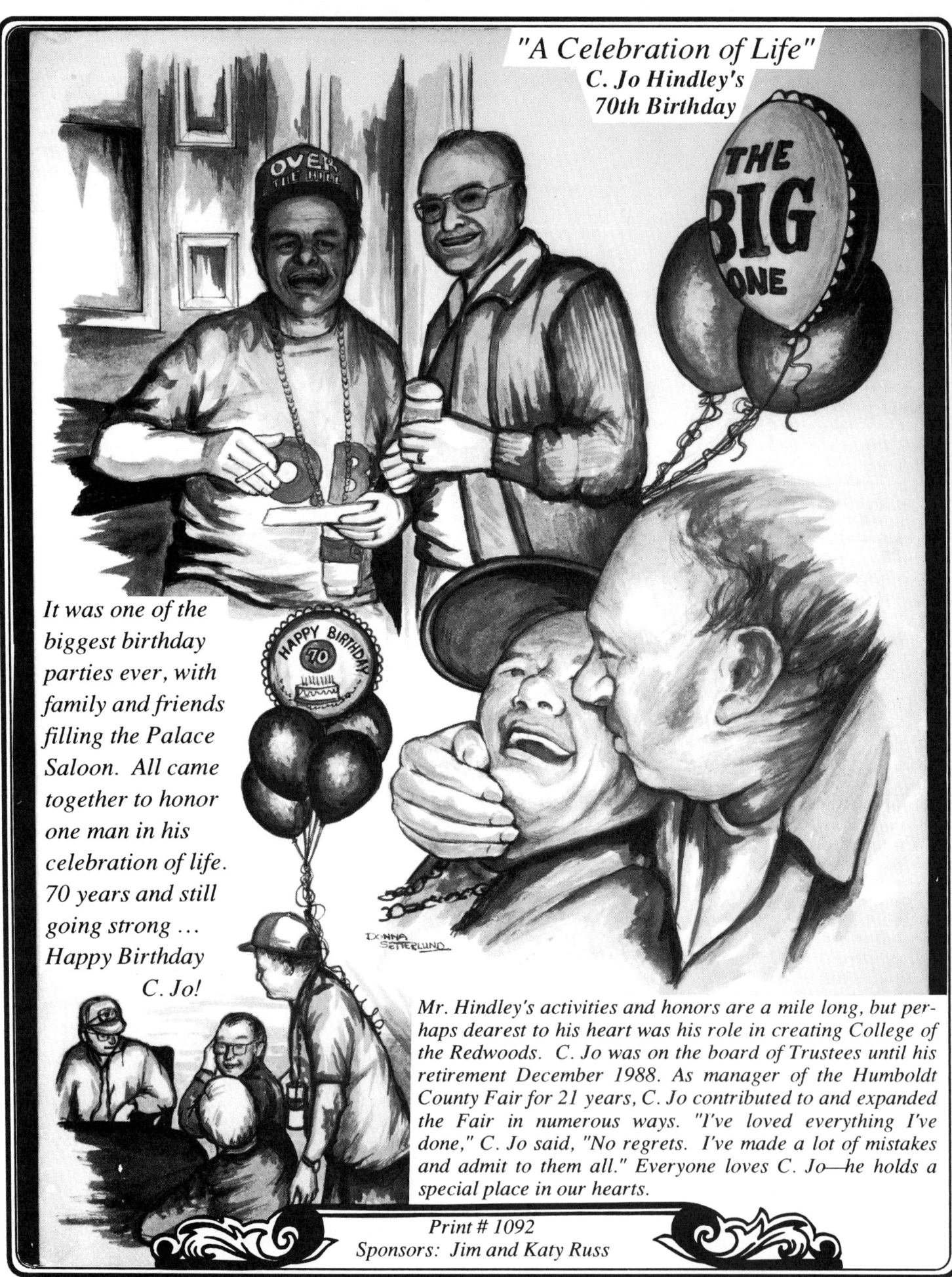

"A Celebration of Life"
C. Jo Hindley's 70th Birthday

It was one of the biggest birthday parties ever, with family and friends filling the Palace Saloon. All came together to honor one man in his celebration of life. 70 years and still going strong ... Happy Birthday C. Jo!

Mr. Hindley's activities and honors are a mile long, but perhaps dearest to his heart was his role in creating College of the Redwoods. C. Jo was on the board of Trustees until his retirement December 1988. As manager of the Humboldt County Fair for 21 years, C. Jo contributed to and expanded the Fair in numerous ways. "I've loved everything I've done," C. Jo said, "No regrets. I've made a lot of mistakes and admit to them all." Everyone loves C. Jo—he holds a special place in our hearts.

Print # 1092
Sponsors: Jim and Katy Russ

"Evo Lourenzo, Acct."

Evo graduated from Humboldt State University in June 1951 and worked in an office at Olsen Implement Co., located in the Village Inn, from July 1951 to March 1954, He got his accounting license in Nov. 1951. On April 1, 1954 he started at Jack Tipple Motors in the office at its present location. In 1965 Evo purchased Citizens Furniture Co. with Richard Tomisini. Rich passed away in 1969 and the furniture store closed in 1970. Evo then went full time into the Accounting Office at 430 Main Street, its present location, and became a Notary Public in 1974.

As Evo continued his career he passed the Internal Revenue Service examination in 1981 and then became an Enrolled Agent for Income Tax. As you walk down Main Street you're likely to see Evo sitting at his desk.

Print # 1093
Sponsor: Lourenzo

"A Small Town Doctor"
#64 The Ferndale Surgery - Ray H. Wiser, M.D.

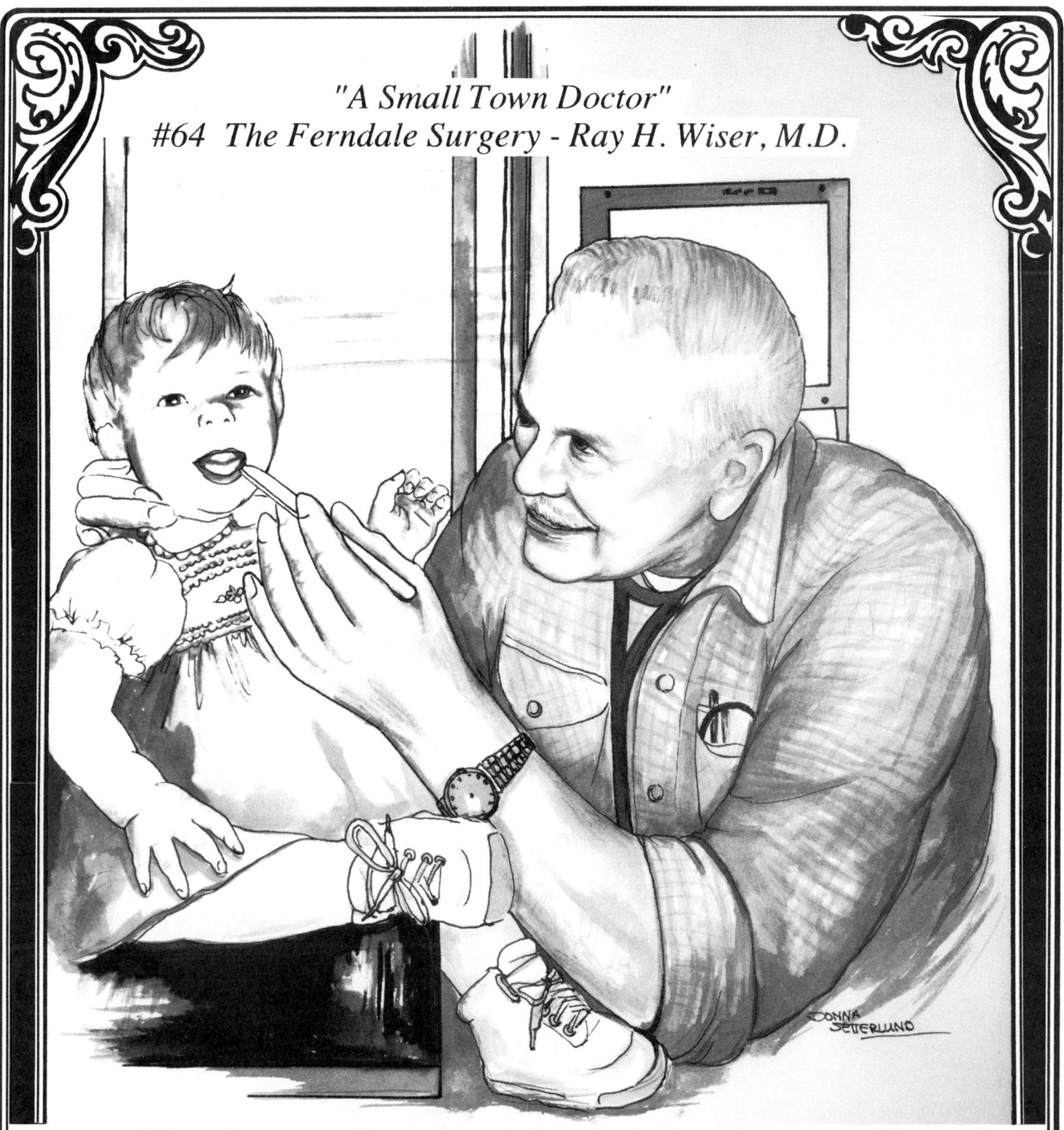

"I have been a small town person since the day I was born on my folks ranch in the Manzanita district near Gridley, California. I was raised on a small peach ranch, and have always enjoyed the personal contact with neighboring patients, farmers, and friends. I guess the old adage of 'You can take the kid out of the country, but not the country out of the kid' fits both my wife and myself. Ferndale is a beautiful place full of beautiful people." Pictured here with Dr. Wiser is Ashliegh Ann Diehl, 8 months old, daughter of Michael and Nina Diehl.

Print # 1095
Sponsor: The Ferndale Surgery

"Around Town"

Some of the folks in our town are really a part of our tradition. Here are a few of these wonderful people. We are proud to introduce them to you.

"Chris" Mathes

Chris can be found at Mathes Jewlery store repairing clocks or putting that personal touch on fine jewelry.

Sponsor: Mathes Jewlers

"Mary" Fisher

Born and raised in Ferndale, Mary has lived here all her life. A Graduate of Ferndale High School in 1943 and employed by Rings Pharmacy since 1965, Mary says, "I love kids!"

Sponsor: Cliff Setterlund

"John"
Affectionately referred to by our townsfolk as "the Walking Man", John Minetta can be seen daily around town. He says he has slowed down to only 7 or 8 miles a day, but still walks at a brisk pace.

"Trudy"
With a constant friendly smile and a warm hello, Trudy is loved by our children and has made friends with each and every one of them. She keeps a gallery of photos of generations of kids who have come into her shop for a treat or just to talk with someone who shows lots of interest in them.

Sponsors: Ferndale Children & Carriage House Studio

"Four O'clock Coffee Club"

Most afternoons a special group of area ranchers, businessmen, and friends meet to discuss important and not so important matters over a cup or two of coffee. Topics may range from who brought in the most hay to who knows what. It doesn't really matter what is discussed as long as the friends are able to get together and share a piece of their day.

Community ties and social gatherings are important to our people. Old friendships and new are made stronger as time is shared, treasured memories re-lived and plans for the future made.

Print # 1098
*Sponsors: **Clancy Adams***
Glen Martella, Tony Rocha

"Friendly Faces"

Print # 1099
Sponsor: Cliff & Donna Setterlund

"Strong Roots"

The Lourenzo (Lorenzo) family were early settlers in Ferndale and many relatives still live in the area. Great grandmother Lourenzo cooked the first Holy Ghost Celebration meals in Portuguese Hall. Sixty five years later her recipes are still used. She is seen here holding her great-granddaughter Debbie Renner. She lived to be 103 and her four sister all lived to be over 100.

Great Grandmother Lourenzo's son John, pictured here, died in 1988 at 94 and two of his sons, Tony and Lionel (Sam) are still active Ferndalers.

Print # 1100
Sponsor: Tony & Dorothy Lorenzo

"Our Teachers"
Thanks for all the extra things you do and the special times you share.

Print # 1101
Sponsors: Cynthia & Shannon George, Jeremy Setterlund

"Dave"

Dave's saddlery is the last of the western stores in northern California that still makes their own saddle, tack, and pack equipment. You'll find Dave Clowes in the very back of the store working on his custom leather products. He's not fast but steady and for godsake don't touch his tools. Dave uses only the finest vegetable-tanned leather and latigo, he throws in a lot of love and know how and comes up with the finest products around. Dave has also been restoring leather equipment that dates back to the early 1900's and he proudly carries on a tradition of doing things the old fashioned way.

Print # 1102
Sponsors: Jim & Penny Ferry

"Hobart"
One of Ferndale's most eccentric characters with a heart as big as the world he loves.

Print # 1103
Sponsor: Cliff & Donna Setterlund

"Our Children"

Our children are our most valued resource. These are our children and we are proud and happy parents. The trials of parenthood find their rewards in the smiles on their faces and the love shared.

Sponsor: Cliff and Donna Setterlund

"A Friendly Welcome & Farewell"

Ady and Myrt Setterlund, life-long residents of Ferndale, have family here dating back to its beginning. Living across from the Humboldt County Fair Grounds and having been back gate keeper for 20 years, Ady greets friends and visitors as they travel to and fro. You may see them on sunny days working in their garden or sitting on the porch waving to passers-by. Ady says from time to time someone will stop and ask him if this is where they sign up to camp at the fairgrounds. He just laughs, wishes them welcome and sends them down to the main office. Wave hello as you pass by.

Print # 1105
Sponsor: The Setterlund Family

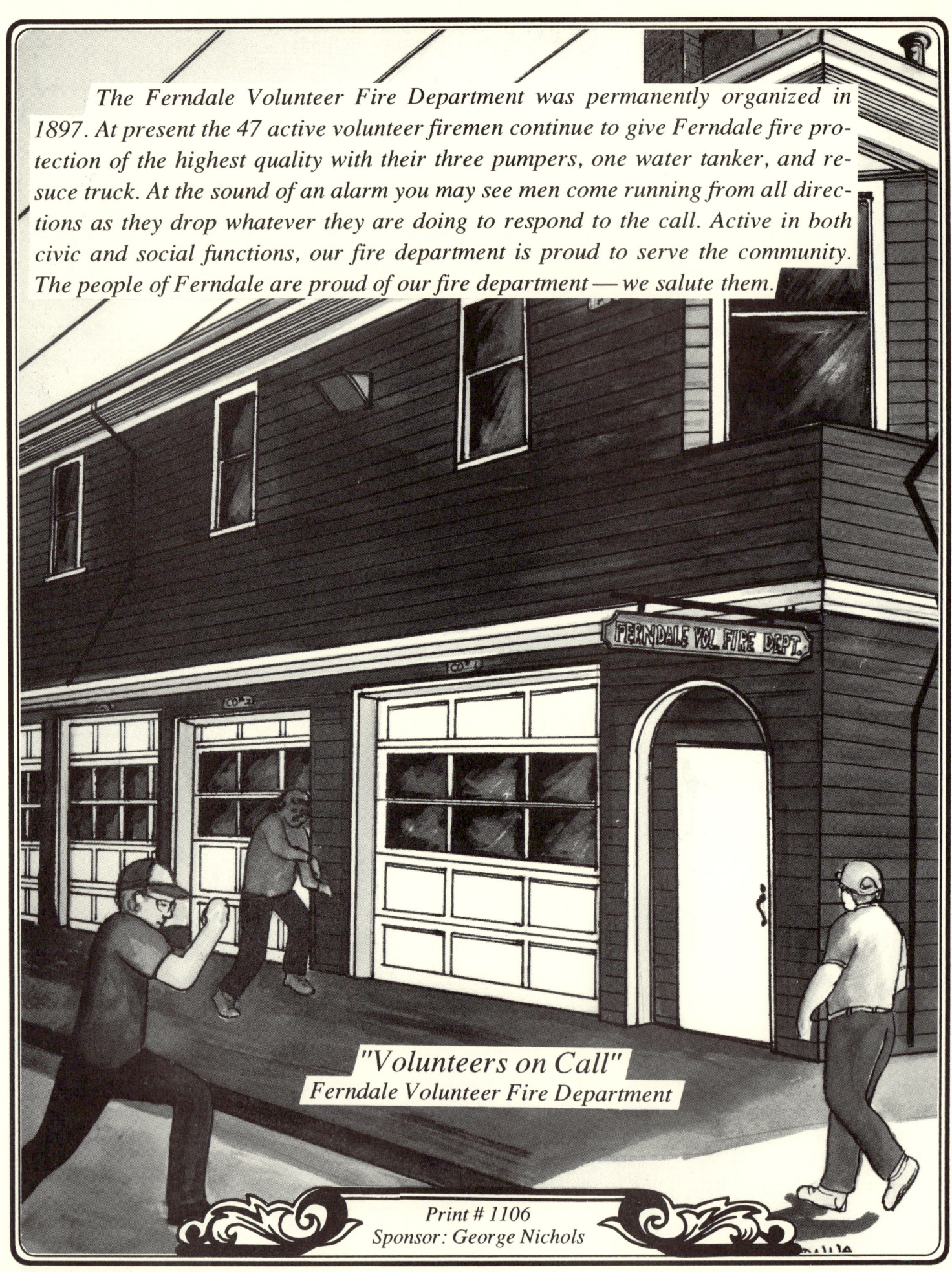

The Ferndale Volunteer Fire Department was permanently organized in 1897. At present the 47 active volunteer firemen continue to give Ferndale fire protection of the highest quality with their three pumpers, one water tanker, and resuce truck. At the sound of an alarm you may see men come running from all directions as they drop whatever they are doing to respond to the call. Active in both civic and social functions, our fire department is proud to serve the community. The people of Ferndale are proud of our fire department — we salute them.

"Volunteers on Call"
Ferndale Volunteer Fire Department

Print # 1106
Sponsor: George Nichols

Chapter 5
"What's Cookin'?"

A tasteful guide to good eating, restaurants, candy shops, or where to get a quick snack.

	Print number	Page number
GUIDE: to good eating		108
Roman's Restaurant	1109	109
The Victorian Village Inn		
Henry Ford's Tavern and Oyster Bar	1110	110
The Victorian Village Inn Restaurant	1111	111
Ferndale Bakery	1112	112
Fern Cafe	1113	113
Ferndale Meat Company	1114	114
Angelina Inn	1115	115

GUIDE: "Good Eating"

#1 **Victorian Village Inn**
Henry Ford's Tavern and Oyster Bar
featuring: Californian, American Cuisine. (Reservations Advised).
400 Ocean Ave., Ferndale .... (707) 785-9400

#5 **Roman's Restaurant**
featuring: Authentic Mexican and American Food
Sunday Fiesta Champagne Brunch
315 Main St., Ferndale .... (707) 725-6358

#20 **The Greek Investment Co. — "Beckers"**
featuring: Cafe & Gathering place for men.
409 Main St., Ferndale .... (707) 786-4180

#38 **Ferndale Bakery**
featuring: Breads, Pastries, Sandwiches, and Refreshments.
543 Main St., Ferndale .... (707) 786-4741

#41 **Red Front Store**
featuring: Quick Snacks, 7 days a week.
577 Main St., Ferndale .... (707) 786-9611

#48 **Fern Cafe**
featuring: Hamburgers, Sandwiches, Shakes, Malts, Softdrinks.
Breakfast, Lunch, Dinner, 7 days a week. Bill and Patty Thielman.
606 Main St., Ferndale .... (707) 786-4795

#60 **Sweetness and Light**
featuring: Traditional Chocolates and Candies.
554 Main St., (next to Post Office), Ferndale ..... (707) 786-4403

#65 **Trudy's Sweets and Treats**
featuring: Bon Bonere Icecream and Candy for kids.
Main St., Ferndale

#76 **Ferndale Meat Company**
featuring: Delicious Meat Sandwiches, Deli Salads, and Soft Drinks.
376 Main St., Ferndale .... (707) 786-4501

#129 **Angelina Inn**
featuring: Prime Rib, Steaks, Seafood & Italian Dinners - just over Fernbridge from Ferndale.
281 Fernbridge Dr., Fernbridge .... (707) 725-3153

#5 "Romans"

Rafael and Benita Roman arrived in Humboldt County in 1959 with a dream. They had a desire to someday serve their homemade Mexican specialties to the public just like Grandma Carmen did in the old country. So, in June of 1983, Roman's Restaurant was born, and features the finest Mexican food in Humboldt County, located at 315 Main Street in the Ivanhoe Building. Lunch and dinners are served in your choice of two large dining rooms.

The specialties feature homemade and daily prepared corn and flour tortillas, fresh homemade soups, beef and chicken fillings, pork ribs, prawns, tomales, flan, fried bananas for desert! And, of course, American Food. Also join us for our Sunday Fiesta Champagne Brunch.

Print # 1109
Sponsor: Rafael and Benita Roman

#2 The Victorian Village Inn

Henry Ford's Tavern, Oyster Bar, and Restaurant are complete with period automobile memorabilia, and two faithfully restored antique Fords. The building also holds an antique Ford automobile museum on the ground floor. With seating of 110, a banquet room seating 100, a banquet & conference room seating 50, the Inn is a popular gathering place for locals, offering reasonably priced fare at lunch and dinner seven days a week. Saturday and Sunday the Inn serves a wonderful brunch featuring their great platter breakfast, eggs benedict, fritattas, and the create your own omelettes made from a long list of ingredients.

The lunch and dinner menu lists appetizers, burgers, salads, and sandwiches, as well as entrees of fine steaks and prime rib, fresh seafood or pasta. Food service is complimented by a full bar with an excellent wine list, champagnes and a wide variety of beers.

Print # 1110
Sponsor: Victorian Village Inn

"Restaurant Dining Room"

Print #1111
Sponsor: Victorian Village Inn

#38 "Ferndale Bakery"

Dan and Cindy Weeks have owned and operated Ferndale Bakery for the past 8 years. Both had been full time bakers before they married and decided to put their knowledge together and open the best Bakery Shop in Humboldt County. Their lifetime experience as bakers has made the bakery state of the art in a variety of baked goods.

They specialize in traditional American baking, including at least 25 different varieties of breads. All bakery items are baked from scratch and contain no preservatives or additives.

As you stroll Main Street in Ferndale, look in the Bakery window and see the overwhelming variety of cookies, pies, muffins, donuts, rolls, breads, and of course decorative cakes for all occassions.

Print # 1112
Sponsors: Dan and Cindy Weeks

#48 "Fern Cafe"

The Fern Cafe, located on the corner of Main and Shaw, has been around for ... well, as far back as I can remember. Having gone through several owners, it is now owned by Bill Thielman and Patty Purvis-Thielman who carry on the tradition of offering home cooking and the best cheeseburger around. Open daily, you can enjoy breakfast, lunch or dinner and choose from milkshakes to home made pies. Relax in their homey atmosphere and let the friendly people at the Fern Cafe serve you in a small town tradition.

Print # 1113
Sponsor: Bill Thielman

#76 Ferndale Meat Company

A meat market has been at this location for over 100 years. The present building, built in 1903, was open at each end and covered with screens to allow cooling of the hanging meat. The original iron hanging racks are still in use as is the original two story smoke house.

Much of the equipment has changed over the years, but the needs of the community are still similar to yesteryear.

Ferndale Meat Company still specializes in custom cutting beef, pork, and lamb from local ranchers. Located in the middle of Ferndale, we offer delicious Meat Sandwiches, choice meats, custom cutting and wrapping, old fashioned sugar curing and smoking, ranch butchering, and frozen food storage lockers.

Print # 1114
Sponsor: Gary Edgmond

#129 "Angelina Inn" Restaurant and Lounge

Located just across Fernbridge, bordering the beautiful banks of the Eel River Valley lies the charming restaurant, the Angelina Inn. Owners John and Shaaron Cardoza took over in July of 1988 and turned the restaurant into the beauty it is today, complete with a fabulous new menu, serving both lunches and dinners, along with banquet facilities and live music on weekends. They have a delicious sample of daily specials from fresh seafood, caught locally, to prime rib and lasagna that has built up quite a reputation, and is known as "second best to none." They are open seven days a week to serve you, and are always cheerful and courteous.

Print # 1115
Sponsor: John and Shaaron Cardoza

Chapter 6
"A Place for the Night"

Bed & Breakfast Inns, Motels, Hotels, and where to park your trailer

— Index —

	Print Number	Page Number
GUIDE: Places to Stay	1117	117
Village Inn Hall (Upstairs)	1118	118
Village Inn (Rooms)	1119	119
Lost Coast Ranch	1120	120
Lost Coast Ranch (Sitting Room)	1121	121
Lost Coast Ranch (Rooms)	1122	122
Francis Creek Inn	1123	123
Ferndale Inn	1124	124
Ferndale Inn (Suite)	1125	125
Shaw House	1126	126
Shaw House (Parlor)	1127	127
Gingerbread Mansion	1128	128

GUIDE: "A Place for the Night"

#1 Victorian Village Inn

Historic rooms & suites, Tavern & Oyster Bar, Dining House & Antique Car Museum. (A.E., M.C. & VISA) Reservations advised.

    400 Ocean Ave., Ferndale, CA 95536 ....(707) 786-9400

#134 Lost Coast Guest Ranch

Offers a full service location for your company's business meetings, training seminars, corporate retreats, hunting or fishing groups or a quiet place for a special family reunion. (A.E., M.C. & VISA) Reservations necessary.

    P.O. Box 1028, Ferndale, CA 95536 ....(707) 786-9400

#45 The Ferndale Inn, Bed & Breakfast

Enjoy a glimpse of the past and relax in one of five comfortable rooms. Continental Plus Breakfast. Reservations advised.

    619 Main Street, Box 887, Ferndale, CA 95536 ....(707) 786-4307

#108 The Shaw House Inn, Bed & Breakfast

Five rooms nestled on the second floor of an elegant Carpenter's Gothic Victorian. Continental Plus Breakfast. Reservations advised.

    703 Main Street, Box 1125, Ferndale, CA 95536 ....(707) 786-9958

#42 Francis Creek Inn

Newly built motel featuring spacious non-smoking rooms in a Victorian decor. Reservations advised.

    557 Main Street, Ferndale, CA 95536 ....(707) 786-9611

#89 The Gingerbread Mansion

Nine elegantly large, romantically Victorian guest rooms. Spectacular private baths, home made breakfast.

    400 Berding Street, Ferndale, CA 95536 ....(707) 786-4000

#124 R.V. Facilities — Humboldt County Fairgrounds

Approximately 75 hook-ups which include water, electricity and access to the sanitary dump station. Special accommodations made for recreational vehicle groups - large or small.

    Fifth Street, Ferndale, CA 95536 ....(707) 786-9511

"Victorian Village Inn"
Upstairs Hall

Print # 1118
Sponsor: Victorian Village Inn

The rooms of the Inn are located on the second floor and are decorated in the American Victorian style of the historic building. There are four beautifully appointed suites and 12 designer-decorated rooms, all with private baths. Luxurious touches include brass beds, elegant armoirs, and goose down comforters.

Print # 1119
Sponsor: Victorian Village Inn

Lost Coast Guest Ranch

The Lost Coast Guest Ranch offers a full service location for your company's business meetings, training seminars, corporate retreats, or a gathering place for your hunting or fishing group. Also a quiet place for a special family reunion.

A working ranch since the 1800's, the ranch is positioned 15 minutes southwest of Victorian Ferndale along the edge of the Pacific. The lodge has been placed on the crest above the private beach to take advantage of the view.

You can relax and do nothing while you are our guest, or you can choose from several activities.

Print # 1120
Sponsor: Lost Coast Guest Ranch

The rooms are all designer-decorated; the main floor has a central living room with a fireplace, satellite dish TV, player piano, and cozy chairs and couches for the whole gang. There is an attractive dining room, and off the large country kitchen is a patio with picnic tables and barbecue pit with a panoramic view of the mountains and ocean.

Our chefs are experts at French country cuisine and will cook wild game when it is available. For groups we can make country platter breakfasts with farm-fresh ingredients, picnic hampers which include fine wine, and old time barbecues or clam and lobster bakes.

Arrangements can be made for our guest to dine at our popular sister resort, the Victorian Village Inn, in nearby Ferndale.

Print # 1121
Sponsor: Lost Coast Guest Ranch

"Lost Coast Ranch Resort"

Off the dining room is a large billiard room with an antique table.

Our 13 luxury rooms and 2 suites offer rustic ranch decor and all have private baths.

You will sleep soundly in the fresh ocean air and stay warm under cozy country quilts.

Print # 1122
Sponsor: Lost Coast Guest Ranch

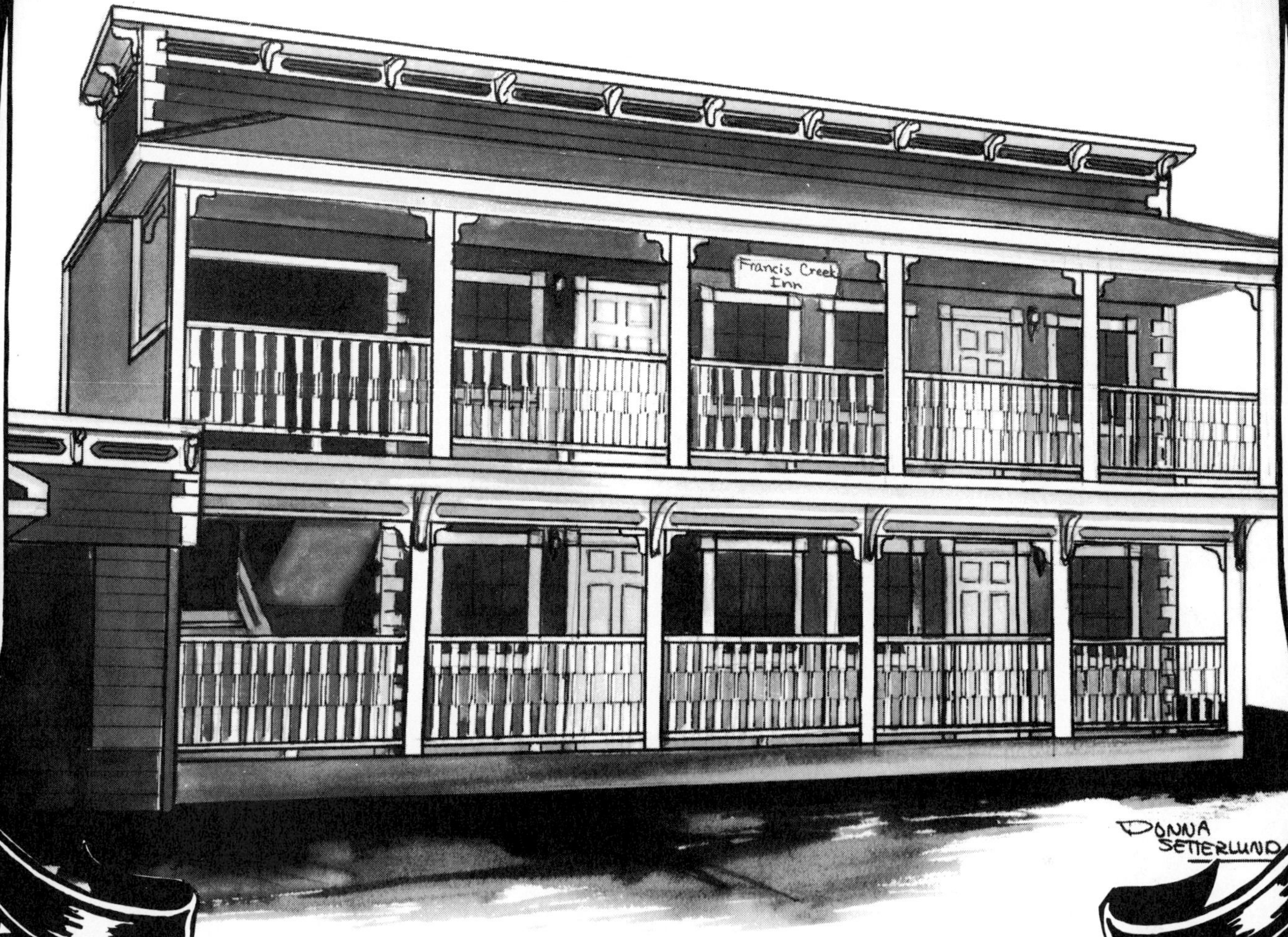

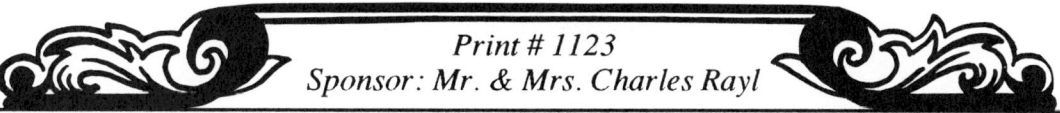

"Francis Creek Inn"

This beautiful Inn is situated downtown in the Victorian Village of Ferndale. Located on the corner of Shaw and Main Streets, this newly built motel features spacious non-smoking rooms in a Victorian decor, comfortable queen sized beds, private baths with tub/shower combinations and color cable television.

The Francis Creek Inn also offers off-street parking. For their guests' convenience they have ice and complimentary coffee in the office.

Print # 1123
Sponsor: Mr. & Mrs. Charles Rayl

"The Ferndale Inn"

The Ferndale Inn was originally the residence of the Fern Dale farm manager and provides another glimpse into the Villages' Victorian past.

Linked by enclosed passageways, the three-building complex borders a central courtyard and promises an evening of pleasant respite for a weary traveler.

Managed by Jim and Danielle McManamon, the inn is resplendant with details of a bygone era. The entire inn is decorated with antiques, handcrafted furnishings, and collectables faithful to the areas' historic character.

Print # 1124
Sponsor: Jim and Danielle McManamon

Ferndale Inn - Bridal Suite

Print # 1125
Sponsor: Jim and Danielle McManamon

"The Shaw House Inn"

Built in 1854 by the founder of Ferndale, the Shaw House has been a gracious guest house since the days when Justice Shaw married and then invited the newlyweds to spend their honeymoon in his master bedroom.

Innkeepers Norma and Ken Bessingpas offer tea in the library at check-in time, and an evening of relaxation as you enjoy the lavish firelit parlor of the Shaw House, now in the National Register of Historic Places. In the morning you will enjoy a Continental Plus breakfast of juice, hot beverages, an innovative and delicious protein dish, and homemade baked goods using local products, along with Olde Fashioned Victorian Goodies, served in the main dining room.

Each of the five guest rooms is set under its own Gothic Gable and is furnished with a private collection of antiques and personal treasures. The Inn sits on an acre of land and features balconies overlooking a secluded creek, and is located only a block away from the Village's Main Street.

Sleeps are deep in this peaceful Victorian community!

Print # 1126
Sponsor: Ken and Norma Bessingpas

Shaw House Inn "Parlor"

Print # 1127
Sponsor: Ken & Norma Bessingpas

"The Gingerbread Mansion"

This distinctive Ferndale landmark was built in 1898. The mansion's unique architectural styling is a combination of Queen Anne and Eastlake Styles. The original building is up front; the rear addition was built in 1920 for a hospital, which was closed after three years for lack of patients. Later it became a rest home, then apartments. Altogether it has 36 rooms on three floors.

The Gingerbread is rich in turned and sawed wood ornament and was named for the elaborate gingerbread trim gracing the building's storybook exterior. Complimenting the architecture is a formal English garden full of two-story high fuchsias, rhododendrons and an unusual topiary.

The mansion features eight guestrooms and two exquisitely furnished parlors and is on the National Register of Historic Places.

Print # 1128
Sponsor: Friends of the Palace

Chapter 7
"Industry, Our Valley, and Other Tidbits"

The dairy industry, ranches, butterfat palaces and other important information.

— Index —

	Print number	Page number
Dairy Industry		130
Humboldt Creamery Association	1131	131
Story of		132
Valley Veterinary	1133	133
Alexandre Dairy	1134	134
Rocha Dairy	1135	135
F&S Leonardo Dairy	1136	136
Losa & Son Dairy	1137	137
Coppini Dairy & Family	1138	138
Ferndale Veterinary	1139	139
Tedsen Home "Butterfat Palace	1140	140
Becker Ranch, Grizzly Bluff Road	1141	141
Carriage House Studio	1142	142
Information About the Prints		143
Order Form		144

Our Dairy Industry & Humboldt Creamery

Along the scenic banks of the Eel River, a group of dedicated dairymen embarked on a cooperative venture. They recognized the fertility of the land in the Ferndale Valley. They brought in dairy herds and, in 1929, formed the Humboldt Creamery Association. They started producing butter and converted the skim milk to casein and liquid whey. Their membership soon covered the deep reaches of the Eel and Van Duzen rivers, and Salmon Creek; then north to Humboldt Bay, Arcata and beyond, and south to Shively and Holmes Flat. In the same year, 1929, they merged with Challenge and were joined by the United Creamery Association of Arcata in 1936. They struggled through the Depression years, yet strived to maintain the high commitment to quality that they still reach today.

Today, Humboldt Creamery Association is 175 Dairymen and an eight-million dollar investment in plant and property. They employ over 70 men and women and play a vital role in their communities. Humboldt Creamery Association produces 2,500,000 gallons of fluid milk, 9,500,000 pounds of butter, 13,000,000 pounds of powder plus 7,500,000 pounds of specialty powders each year. Their products and byproducts are distributed as far as Crescent City in the north and to Garberville, Ruth and Petrolia in the south and east. Humboldt Creamery Association and Challenge products are found in over 100 stores and over 150 fast-food and deli locations throughout Humboldt and Del Norte Counties.

With the addition of the Loleta manufacturing facility in 1985, Humboldt Creamery Association now handles all the milk in Humboldt County. They not only produce and distribute dairy products under the Challenge and Humboldt Creamery labels, but also provide milk to the Loleta Cheese Factory and the Bon Boniere Ice Cream Company.

Today, the Humboldt dairymen are testimony to the fertility of the land. The lumbermen had inherited the patient labors of Nature, the fishermen waited the inscrutable harvest of the sea, but the Humboldt dairy farmers enrich the hand of Nature and the ideas of men in a business democracy rooted deeper in the land than the giant Redwoods.

Sponsors: Rich Losa, Joe Alexandre, Bobbie Coppini, Frank Leonardo

Humboldt Creamery Association
— since 1929 —
"A Commitment to Quality"

Print: # 1131
Sponsor: Humboldt Creamery Assoc.

No one knows for sure when mankind first began to apply healing skills to himself and his animals. Early healers relied on magic and worship to help overcome illness. Long ago, prehistoric man demonstrated his esteem and enigmatic affection for animals in his art. Painting in the caves of Lascaux and Altamira some 10,000 to 15,000 years B.C. are prominent examples of this art which suggest these works were produced as part of a magic ritual, the meaning of which is uncertain. Later, mankind began to acquire basic medical skills among sheep herding people about 9000 B.C. A factual foundation for medicine was laid by cattle people such as the bull-cow culture of Egypt that existed from about 4000 to 300 B.C. Then, the stage for progress shifted to horse-centered societies. A number of the latter societies were transformed into the major economically developed countries of the 20th Century.

The civilization of man evolved from the domestication of animals, namely the cattle. Probably by capturing orphaned auroch calves, man finally succeeded in domesticating some of the wild cattle at least 8000 years ago. Man found that he could dominate the cow, but bulls were another matter, thus some of the more common surgical procedures were developed, specifically nose-ringing, dehorning and castration. From the beginning these animals were too venerated, prestigious, or otherwise valuable for mankind to consider routinely using them as a source of meat. This was particularly true when mankind made the great discovery that a simple wedge pulled by an ox could break the soil far faster and more efficiently for seed sowing than could his digging stick.

The City of Ferndale was founded on the banks of the Eel River much like the early great civilizations of the Fertile Crescent. Cattle cultures, highly advanced for its time, settled along the banks of the Nile, Tigris and Euphrates Rivers to support trading, particularly in cattle, and feeds, such as grain. This close relationship benefitted man in many ways; in developing cultures, societies, language, writing, laws and paved the way for specialized breeds of cattle.

For a long period, the bull horns remained a symbol of Rulers and power throughout the Fertile Crescent. Significantly, the first letter of our alphabet, of Canaanite-Phoenician origin is derived from the cuneiform sign for cattle, alpu in Akkadian, alphu in Hebrew, and in Greek alpha, it is a picture of a cow's head with curved horns on its side; as our letter "A", the pictorgraph has straight horns upsidedown. Certainly, the ancient Fertile Crescent was populated largely by people of cattle cultures. In addition, the cattle culture was evident for Ancient Rome. In fact, Italy, takes its name from Italus, a noble bull chased from Sicily by Hercules.

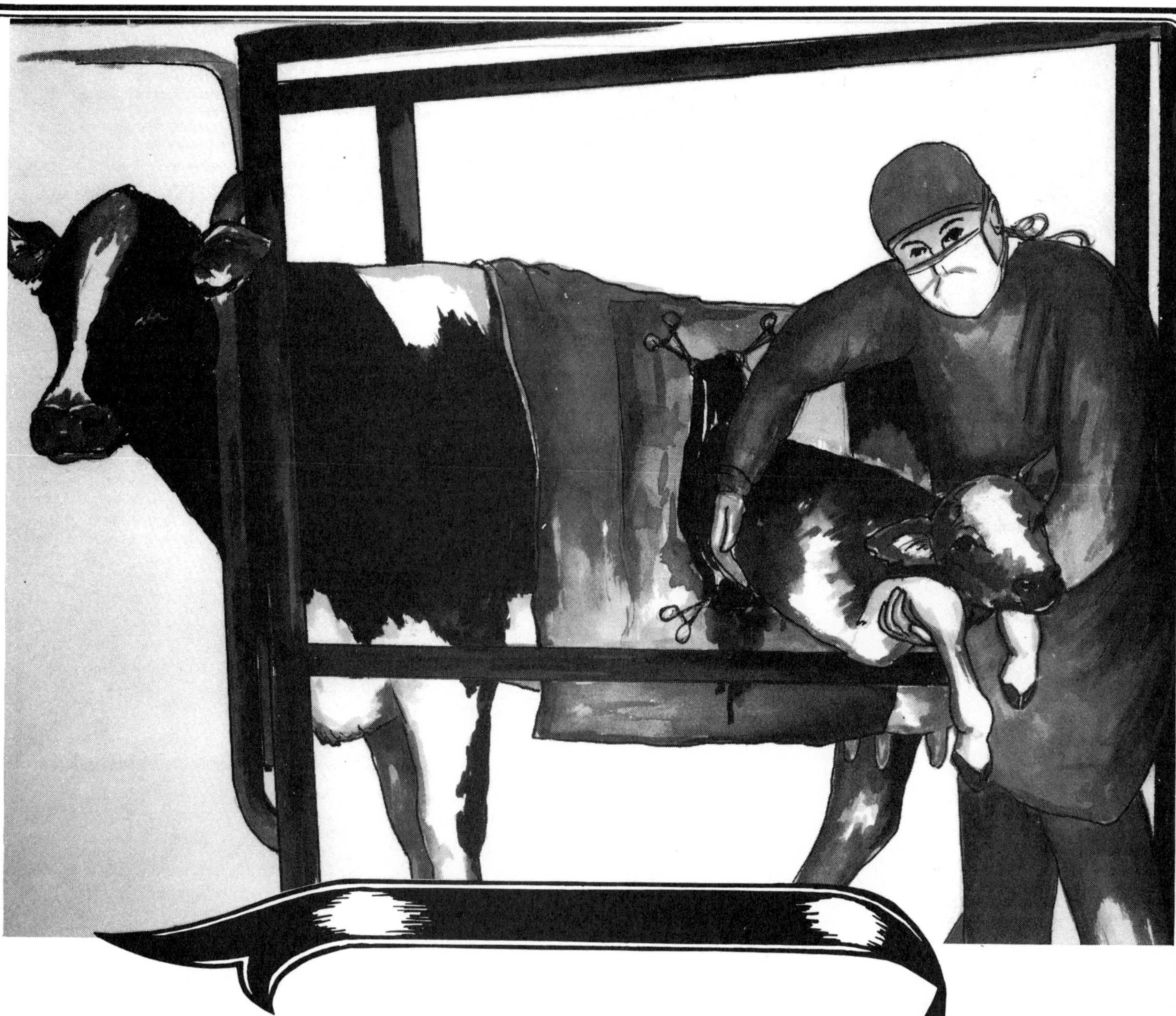

Valley Veterinary

Since earliest times healers have been sought to treat sickness and injury. Modern veterinary practice serves to apply the technicological advances of science and medicine to our domestic and zoological species. The progress in epidemiology, animal production, medical treatment and surgery can be much appreciated in the highly visible surgical intervention as shown here to correct illness. Dr. Joseph A. Humble, adapted from Schwabe, <u>Cattle, Priests and Progress in Medicine, Vol 4</u>, University of Minnesota Press, 1978.

Print # 1133
Sponsor: Joe Humble

Alexandre Dairy

Alexandre Dairy has been in the business since 1961 - milking Holstien cows. Joe was a 12 year old boy when he came to Ferndale from the Azores. It was his dream to have a modern milking barn. That dream was fulfilled in 1976 when a fully automated milking parlor was built.

Joe and his wife, Loretta, raised three three children, Renae, Blake, and Kristina. The Family was honored in 1988 when Alexandre Dairy was named Humboldt County's Dairy of the Year.

Print # 1134
Sponsor: Joe and Loretta Alexandre

"Tony & Lucy Rocha Dairy"

This Dairy Ranch on Fulmor Road was leased to Tony Rocha in 1946 by Mr. & Mrs. Eugene DeCarli. In 1951 Tony and Lucy bought the Grade B Dairy and in later years developed it to a Grade A Dairy. Tony retired January 4, 1989 and the Dairy is now leased to Jay & Margaret Coppini.

Print # 1135
Sponsors: Tony & Lucy Rocha

"F & S Leonardo Dairy"

The Dairy is located in the Grizzly Bluff area sitting on the bank of the mighty Eel River and circled by Grizzly Bluff and East Terry Roads. In the late 1880's and early 1900's, the Eel River had its channel behind the old hay and milking barn. When it returned to its original channel in 1964 it took some 20 acres, before Leonardo's dike was built to retain it.

Frank H. Leonardo, a 2nd generation dairyman, has been on this ranch since February 1957. He purchased it in 1960 when it was a 60 cow Grade B operation. Now it is a 225 Milking Grade A operation and he has gone from 155 acres to 373 acres. Together with his wife Sylvia, they have raised 2 children and next year son Frank J. will be continuing in his father's footsteps and become a 3rd generation dairymen and 2nd on this ranch.

Print # 1136
Sponsor: Frank and Sylvia Leonardo

"Losa and Son Dairy"

John Losa, born in Switzerland, and his wife Rose started dairying in the Camp Weott area of Ferndale in 1939. In 1951 they bought the present dairy at Coffee Creek.

In 1962, their son and daughter in law, Richard and Corinne, bought the business and in 1975 purchased the land.

The Grade A Dairy is now operated as Losa and Son Dairy and is owned by Richard & Corinne Losa and Tom & Cindy Losa.

The Dairy consists of 160 acres of owned and leased land. There are presently 160 Holstein milk cows and numerous young stock. The milk is processed at Humboldt Creamery at Fernbridge.

Print # 1137
Sponsor: Rich and Corinne Losa

Four Generation Coppini's

John W. Coppini was born in Switzerland in 1868. He came to America at 17 years old, and moved to Ferndale in 1889. He bought what is now known as the J.W. Coppini Estate in December of 1902 at $300.00 an acre. He milked 20 cows.

In 1924 Leo, John and Augusta's only son, married Mary Regli. Leo and Mary took over the Dairy in 1938. They had the 1st cow of all breeds to produce over 10,000 lbs of lifetime butterfat. At 16 years old, Francis, the oldest son of Leo and Mary, went to work milking cows for his father. In 1941 Francis moved down the lane to another dairy, where he operated a 50 cow dairy for his father. Five years later he went partners in the Dairy business with his brother Don. Francis married Hilda Machado in 1948. In 1950 Francis and Hilda moved to the Halley place milking 40 cows. In 1955 Francis and Hilda made their final move to Fulmor Road on a Dairy now known as the Coppini Ranch, where they started milking 100 cows. Now, in 1989, the Coppini Ranch is operated by Francis and Hilda along with their son and daughter in law, Bob and Cathy. There are presently 550 cows milked, one half being Jersey and the other Holstein.

Included in the Coppini Family Picture: Mrs. Leo Mary Coppini, Francis and Hilda, Bob and Cathy with their two children Kenny and Jody Coppini.

Print # 1138
Sponsor: Coppini Family

Ferndale Veterinary

History: Ferndale Veterinary originated in 1948 when Drs. Harlan Detlefsen and Melvin Roberts established their veterinary practice. For over 30 years the two doctors maintained the only veterinary practice in Ferndale, named Detlefsen and Roberts, and were instrumental in shaping the agricultural economy of Humboldt County.

Present Use: Ferndale Veterinary is owned by Dr. Charles Ozanian who bought the practice in 1983 upon the retirement of Drs. Deftlefsen and Roberts. The building was enlarged the same year to include a diagnostic laboratory, computer work station, and office. The practice employs one full time veterinarian besides Dr. Ozanian, as well as two licensed Animal Health Technicians. Ferndale Veterinary services ranches and dairy farms throughout Humboldt County as well as companion animals from Ferndale and neighboring communities.

Pring # 1139
Sponsor: Charles Ozanian

"Butterfat Palaces"

Ammer House, built in 1892 by Chris Ammer with the assistance of Henry Rohner, is an excellent example of Carpenter's Art. Mr. Ammer operated a good-sized dairy ranch on his property and had an interest in a nearby creamery as was the case of the owners of so many of these large homes; thus the term "Butterfat Palaces," came into existence.

Butter was the only dairy product that could be preserved; for unknown reasons cheese never became a viable article of commerce. Butter was one of the best and finest means of a "cash crop" or product in Ferndale and other areas of Humboldt County.

The house is presently owned and occupied by Mr. & Mrs. Raymond Tedsen, who continue the tradition as dairymen.

Print # 1140
Sponsor: Mr. & Mrs. Ray Tedsen

"Becker Ranch"
Grizzly Bluff Road

Throughout our valley you will see many ranches such as this one nestled against the hills. The large barns provide shelter for the varied livestock and storage for hay and equipment. Jim and Jacque Becker, who recently purchased this ranch, both come from local families and find Dairying a rewarding lifestyle and business. Take a drive out of Ferndale on our back roads and enjoy the beauty of our picture-perfect countryside.

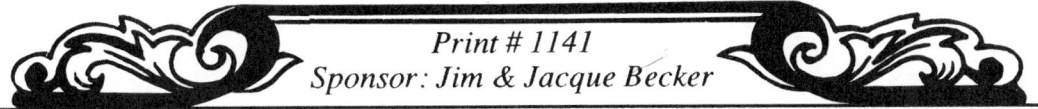

Print # 1141
Sponsor: Jim & Jacque Becker

"Carriage House Studio"

    Return to a Grand Era when the quality of hand crafted workmanship was the mark of excellence.

    In our studio we pride ourselves in offering products that have been made with care. Each is distinctively designed to create a unique piece of beauty, from sand-sculptured Redwood Signs, Etched Glass and Mirrors, to art Publications. Our goal is to recreate the beauty of our heritage with a quality of workmanship you'll be proud to own.

    Our family-operated business believes in old fashioned hard work and honesty. From our wood shop to our art studio we try to create ideas and products of distinction.

Print # 1142
Sponsor: Cliff & Donna Setterlund

About the Prints

The prints offered in this book are fine quality reproductions from original ink and acrylic paintings. Each is matted to your satisfaction and ready for framing.

Specifications:

    Prints: *10" x 14"*

    Paper: *80 lb. Felt*

                  Black & White on antique white paper

    Mat Size: *16" x 20" - $20.00*

    Mat Colors: *Black, Grey, or antique gold*

    Frames   *Custom crafted frames, superb quality*

                  Prints fit in standard 16" x 20" frames

Ordering Information:

    Fill in print number, description, mat color, quantity and price. California residents please add 6% sales tax. Include check or money order. (U.S. funds only). We ship UPS. Please give street address.

— WE GUARANTEE YOUR SATISFACTION —

If for any reason you are not satisfied with your order, please return it to us and we will promptly return your money.

Inquiries regarding original art, books, greeting cards, and limited-edition prints can be made by writing Donna Setterlund, Carriage House Studio Publication, P.O. Box 712, Ferndale, CA 95536

Carriage House Studio Publications
P.O. Box 712
Ferndale, California 95536
(707) 786-4042

Date of Order: _____

Prices: Book $12.95
Map $3.00
Print $20.00
(10" x14" - 16" x 20" matted)

Print No.	Description	Mat Color	Quantity	Price	Extension

Mat Colors:
  Black
  Grey
  Antique Gold

Total Amount
(Calif. Residents) 6% Sales Tax
Shipping & Handling   3.00
Total Amount Enclosed $

Check or money order - Payment should be in U.S. funds

Send to: (please print) _____
Name _____
Address _____
City _____ State _____ Zip _____
Phone (___) _____

Thank you for your order!   *Cliff & Donna Setterlund*